Successfully Buy Your Business:

Expert Advice from a Business Broker

By Andrew Rogerson

Certified Business Intermediary (CBI)
Certified Business Broker (CBB)
Certified Machinery and Equipment Appraiser (CMEA)
Certified Senior Business Analyst (CSBA)

www.Andrew-Rogerson.com

Published by

RBS

Rogerson Business Services
Sacramento, CA
www.businesstransactionbooks.com

Rogerson Business Services
777 Campus Commons Road, Suite 200
Sacramento, CA, 95825
www.businesstransactionbooks.com

Successfully Buy Your Business: Expert Advice from a Business Broker
Copyright © 2008-2009 Andrew Rogerson, CBI, CBB, CMEA, CSBA

ISBN: 978-1-4775455-7-7

Library of Congress Registration Number: TX-7-071-315

Disclaimer

This publication is to educate and provide accurate and helpful information on buying a business. It is sold with the understanding that the author is NOT engaged in offering legal, accounting or any other professional advice. Please consult a competent professional for assistance.

Acknowledgements

Business Brokerage Press
Business Brokerage by Lloyd R Manning
Monty Watson, Walker Advisory Associates
The Business Reference Guide by Tom West
California Association of Business Brokers (CABB)
Len Krick, United Business Brokers, Las Vegas, NV
International Business Brokers Association (IBBA)
Roger Murphy at Murphy Business and Financial Corporation, Clearwater, FL
The Resource Handbook for Business Brokers and Intermediaries by Tom West
Ultimate Guide to Personal Finance for Entrepreneurs by Peter Sander with J Jeff Lambert
Entrance: A Business Owner's Guide to Buying a Business by Alexander Vantarakis & William Whitehurst

Special Thanks

Special thanks to the following for contributing to the text and/or checking the details: John Rogerson, Tony Gilbert, Roger Murphy, Tim Rogers, Greg Roquet, Jerry Tsai and Fred Hall.
Also thanks to Nick Kalfountzos "The Graphics Man."

Extra Special Thanks

An extra special thanks to Anne Rogerson and Belinda Rogerson for reviewing each of the four guides and for their positive and constructive feedback.

Special Acknowledgment of IBBA

The International Business Brokers Association is a global organization that advances the professional development of over 1,800 member intermediaries, educates potential clients about the value of intermediary services, and promotes the highest possible standards of ethical conduct. IBBA sponsors national education programs and conferences twice each year and cooperates with state and local business broker's organizations to conduct "grass roots" programs for the benefit of business communities around the country. IBBA awards the prestigious designation of Certified Business Intermediary (CBI) to members who demonstrate professional excellence through their Intermediary experience and education and pass a comprehensive examination. Andrew Rogerson holds the CBI designation.

For more information contact:

International Business Brokers Association
401 North Michigan Avenue, 24th Floor
Chicago, IL 60611-4267
Phone: 888-686-4222   Fax: 312-673-6599
E-mail: admin@ibba.org
Web: www.ibba.org

Special Acknowledgment of CABB

The California Association of Business Brokers is a professional trade association whose members are actively involved in assisting their clients in buying, selling, and evaluating businesses. CABB exists to recognize the professionals of business opportunity brokerage, to help educate the public on the benefits of using licensed intermediaries, and to establish a code of ethics to which members adhere. CABB awards the prestigious designation of Certified Business Broker (CBB) to members who demonstrate professional excellence through their intermediary and business brokerage experience and education and pass a series of examinations. Andrew Rogerson holds the CBB designation.

For more information contact:

California Association of Business Brokers
1215 K Street, Suite 2290
Sacramento, CA, 95814
Phone: 866-972-2220   Fax: 916-231-2141
E-mail: cabb@cabb.org
Web: www.cabb.org

Table of Contents

Welcome. 2
Your Goals 3
Idea Tracker 4

Section One: General Information

Business Ownership – What Are My Options? 8
How Do I Know If Being A Business Owner Is Right For Me? 10
6 Personality Traits Of An Entrepreneur 13
7 Stages Of The Business Life Cycle 14
Expectations: Seller Vs Buyer 16
7 "Musts" Before Buying Your Business 17
No Dream, No Story, No Song – 8 Dream Killers 18
Passion - Good Or Bad 22

Section Two: Education

Legal Entity Options 26
Fictitious Business Name Or DBA 29
Federal Employer Information Number..30
Business License And Other Licenses And Permits...31
Sales And Use Tax...32
Insurance Options 33
Patents/Trademarks And Copyright...37
Finance Planning Tools..39
Start-Up Expense Planner 40
Sales Forecast...41
Profit And Loss Projection...42
Other Finance Planning Tools 43
Risk Management 44
Finance Options 45
Transaction Documents 47
Stock Sale V Asset Sale 49
Agency 51
Business Valuations 53
Other Types Of Valuations 56
Professionals You Can Hire..57

Section Three: Assess Your Qualifications

Create And Understand Your Buyer Profile...66
Determine Your Down Payment And Borrowing Ability 75
Determine Your Business Experience 75
What You Will Need To Buy Your Business 76
Identify Licensing Requirements..77
Understand Lifestyle Changes 79
Personal Budget Planner 81
Identify Geographic Location 82
Assemble Your Team 82

Section Four: Search for the best business

Search For The Best Business...87
Do I Have The Qualifications And Finances To Enter This Industry?.......90
Review Blind Business Summary...92
Complete And Return The NDA...94
Determine Interest...103
Review Confidential Business Information 103

Section Five: Make a deal

Meet Seller..107
Tour Business...107
Do A Gut Check To Analyze Your Interest Level....................................108
Make An Offer..108
Letter Of Intent, Asset Purchase Agreement Or Stock Offer 109
Negotiate If Necessary - Counter Offers...110

Section Six: Close the deal

Open Due Diligence...116
Due Diligence Checklist 117
Secure Finance...120
Obtain Lender Instructions...121
Close Due Diligence And Open Escrow...122
Lease – New, Assign Or Sub-lease...123
License Requirements – Franchisor/Liquor etc 123
Start The Bulk Sale Process..124
Purchase Price Allocation...125
Sign Final Documents – Close Escrow..126
Create Your Legal Entity..126

Section Seven: Your first 100 days

Grand Opening..129
Business Plan 130
8 Important Functions Of A Business Plan..134
Sales And Marketing Plan...136
Elevator Speech 139
Productivity Plan...140
Value Of A Mentor...142
Tax Planning 143

Section Eight: Additional Information and Tools

SBA Programs And Other Finance Options 147
Recasting Financial Statements 149
Final Checklist 153
Associations Of Interest...155
Additional Sources Of Information 157

Glossary 160

About The Author 168

Welcome

When an entrepreneur first decides to look at business ownership, it generally sets off a series of complex and confusing questions as well as an emotional roller coaster. The complex and confusing questions include…Will I buy an existing business? If it's already an existing business it should come with an established with a customer base, trained employees, and business procedures thereby lowering your risk. What about buying a franchise? This may be easier as I then have the franchisor to help me? How about I start my own business, I can then do it my way? If I start my own business, what will I do and will it be successful? The bottom line is that it's already pretty confusing and hard to decide.

As we've seen above, business ownership has three different paths, however, this workbook is built for one purpose only and that is to help a business owner who is considering buying their own business. Lots of would-be entrepreneurs go down the path of looking to buy or start their own business. Many stop before they really get going, while many start but don't conclude the journey as they run out of time, money, enthusiasm or all of these reasons combined, or for other reasons. If your preference is to start your own business, a separate workbook is available called Successfully Start Your Business: Expert Advice from a Business Broker. If your decision is to buy a franchise then please look for my workbook called Successfully Buy Your Franchise: Expert Advice from a Business Broker.

If this workbook has one purpose it has two goals. The first goal is to outline and inform the different tasks and questions a business buyer will ask as they move through the decision making process. The second goal is to encourage you, as the business buyer, once you buy your business, to use your first 100 days to build solid processes and put systems and strategies in place so your business settles and grows with you as the new owner. Perhaps I can hear you gasp – that doesn't make much sense, but obviously I beg to differ.

The inspiration for this guide comes from my personal experiences in buying, selling, owning, and operating five businesses in two countries, researching many, many different types of businesses, and my current experience as a business consultant/broker to those that wish to enter or exit business ownership. I wish someone had given me some organized structure to tackle this difficult experience as I have had to learn it the hard way. Now my goal is to help make that journey easier for you.

Please use this workbook to make notes along the way. This is a guide to read, learn, and stimulate. Scribble ideas and inspirations you have and check them out later so you don't lose your thoughts and are therefore ultimately better prepared. If you prefer to make lots of notes before finalizing your thoughts, photocopy the pages so you can have one final version to work through as you arrive at different decision points.

Buying an existing business requires skill, patience, courage, money, and good old fashioned hard work. So be patient as you travel your journey…though without question, the rewards are wonderful. And I wish you nothing but success.

Your Goals

Use the chart below to write down major tasks that come to mind that you feel you must do to successfully buy your business. Refer back to this chart as you read through this guide so that you can add tasks you want to complete and stay up-to-date.

Task Description	Start Date	Completion Date

Idea Tracker

As you read this guide, hopefully it will inspire ideas or prompt action items. Use the space below to jot down and track these ideas so you can organize your thoughts into action items.

Your Feedback

The goal of this guide is to help new or potential business owners through the process of buying their business in the quickest time possible for the best price possible. Although all new business owners have the same objective when buying their business, the journey to achieving that goal is never the same.

There are a wide variety of factors that affect the entire process:

- ✓ Buyers and Sellers have unique personal differences.
- ✓ The professional support services each party hires may come into conflict.
- ✓ The direction of the economy has impact beyond anyone's control.
- ✓ The current state of the industry the business is a part of can have a positive or a negative impact.
- ✓ Taxes and related laws often change.

Because of these factors and many others, I strongly advise you to seek the assistance of experts when it comes time to actually buying a business.

If you have comments or suggestions that you feel would improve this guide and you have a moment to share, please e-mail your suggestions to info@andrew-rogerson.com.

With thanks,

Andrew Rogerson

The Golden Rule
The Golden Rule when buying a business is to put yourself in the shoes of the seller and see things from their perspective.

Section One

General Information

"Education is the ability to meet life's situations."

Dr. John G. Hibben

Introduction

The steps to buying an established business are numerous, almost always complex, and at times, very frustrating. Most of the decisions are logical and straightforward and sequential, that is, you can only go from A to C via B. As I said in the Welcome, the major purpose of this guide is to help a buyer or potential buyer through the process of buying an existing business. Buying, owning, and operating a business is not for everyone. But hopefully following these steps, it will allow you to make that determination on your own, as there are great personal, financial, and emotional rewards in business ownership.

Additionally, this guide is written from a different perspective. It is not written from the perspective of an accountant, attorney, financial planner, business coach, landlord or employee, but that of a business broker. My current profession is that of a business broker. I help business owners exit business ownership or buyers enter business ownership. I get into the nitty gritty of a business and see what's happening, what's done well, what could be done better, and how both sides in the transaction can see things differently. My job is to bring everyone together. It is this perspective I bring to this guide. The questions I ask, the processes I suggest, and the dynamic I bring, also comes from my business brokering experience.

Remember, this guide is built for work. Make notes and use the templates to jot down ideas as they come to mind so you can refer back to them. The buying of your business is unique. One of the main reasons for publishing this in workbook format is so that you can write in it, customize, and use the information to be successful in buying your business in the quickest time possible.

The flow of the guide is as follows:
- ✓ Section One provides some general information on some of the concepts and terms you may come across when buying a business.
- ✓ Section Two educates on different skills, terms, language and personnel you may need.
- ✓ Section Three gets you to focus on how you need to prepare as the buyer so you can present yourself effectively in the transaction as well as incorporate some of the topics covered earlier.
- ✓ Sections Four, Five and Six deal with the process of buying your business.
- ✓ Section Seven makes some suggestions about how to go about your first 100 days of business ownership so you build solid foundations.
- ✓ Section eight concludes with some additional resources and tools that may be of interest to you as you work through the variables of buying your business.

Please write down any terms you come across that aren't familiar to you. At the back of this guide there is a glossary that defines some terms you may come across. If they aren't covered in the glossary, you are welcome to e-mail them to me at info@Andrew-Rogerson.com and I will add them to the next edition of the guide. You are also welcome to e-mail questions about buying your business.

Business Ownership – What Are My Options?

So you're considering buying a business and calling it your own. Before we get too deep into that, let's have a look at your options. Basically there are only three options. First, start a business from scratch with your own idea, second, buy the rights to a franchise system and become a franchisee, or look for an existing business for sale so you can operate and manage it.

Below is a table that captures each of the three options and then attempts to lay out the different risks or variables associated with each idea. I've included this table to give you some talking or thinking points to see if you can find one option that makes more sense to you than the other. The list below is not exhaustive so please use the table on the next page to add other ideas that are important to you. It may create action items for you to research further so write them down as well. If you have questions, challenges, suggestions or simply want to vent, please email me at info@andrew-rogerson.com

	Start new business	*Buy existing business*	*Buy a franchise*
Availability	None	Limited	Many
Established business methodologies	None	Hopefully	Yes
Documented processes	None	Limited - if at all	Yes
Training	None	Initial 2 weeks or so	Initial and ongoing
Investment V Profit	None	Yes	None
Support during ownership	None	None	Yes
Risk	Highest	Unknown until you're the owner	Many variables
Finance availability	Very difficult	Yes	Yes
How to predict success	Success based on projections	Success comes from history only	Success based on feedback from current owners
Decision maker	Owner	Owner	Follow the system
Instant cash flow	No	Yes	No
Established customer relationships	No	Yes	No
Established relationship with suppliers	No	Yes	Maybe
Established reputation	No	Yes	Yes
Established brand	No	Yes	Yes

Use the table below to write down additional ideas you consider important to include when deciding which business option to pursue

Idea	Start new business	Buy existing business	Buy a franchise

Write down any ideas you want to research further.

How Do I Know If Being A Business Owner Is Right For Me?

This is possibly a burning question as you consider different options, especially if what you are currently doing is not rewarding and you want to do something else. What are your options? Do you find a new job, stay in your current position or do you move into business ownership? As you look for answers to these questions, I suggest there may be many suggestions from those around you, but ultimately the final answer has to come from you and you alone. Deciding if buying an existing business and therefore business ownership is right for you, includes many emotions and motivations. Consider the following:

- ✓ No more layoffs
- ✓ Having control of your work and personal life
- ✓ Having balance with work, family and friends
- ✓ Financial security
- ✓ Personal fulfillment
- ✓ Success
- ✓ Creating and building something
- ✓ Contributing to the community
- ✓ Family involvement
- ✓ No company politics
- ✓ Less frustration and job stress
- ✓ Getting away from corporate life

And perhaps I forgot the most important one – money. I think a major reason most people enter business ownership is because they believe they can make more money than what they currently doing and perhaps in the foreseeable future. What's interesting is that according to the book, the Millionaire Next Door, five out of six millionaires do so through business ownership.

How else do I decide?

Part of the purpose of this guide is to take you through the process so you can decide if starting a business from scratch makes sense to you. That's the purpose of this guide or work book and that is, allowing you to arrive at the decision that makes sense to you. Not your spouse. Not your parents, family, best friend, neighbor, accountant, mentor, coach, consultant or advisor…but YOU.

But here are some other things to consider:

Goals

I think you would agree that all successful people have goals. I suspect that even unsuccessful people have goals, they perhaps lack the discipline, risk management skills, organizational skills, personal drive, education, and chutzpah or perhaps they are unlucky. Or maybe they are on the path to success but just haven't got there yet. Whatever, if you've decided business ownership is something you want to consider I expect the underlying drive is that you have goals and you see business ownership as the means to get there, but one of the underlying goals you have is personal wealth.

Entrepreneur V Intrapreneur

In the Welcome on page 7 we mentioned the three ways of entering business ownership – buy an existing business, buy the rights to a franchise or start a business from scratch. (Yes, can you can buy an existing franchise but that's covered by option two.)

Perhaps the way to work out the best option for you is by a process of elimination. The key ingredients I would suggest to successfully **buy an existing business** include:

1. Motivation to go into business ownership but don't have a new business idea or an improvement on an existing idea. Your thought is to buy an existing business and either radically improve it by turning it around, find a business that is ready to go to the next level but needs some Tender Loving Care or simply take a business that is currently performing well and maintain that business as it provides a steady income for you and your family.
2. The money to fund your business purchase, borrow against the business and keep you fed, clothed and housed.
3. The business skills to see a good opportunity to manage not only the employees and keep the existing customers happy but also manage the sales and marketing, operation, management, and financial systems of the business to make or continue its profitability.
4. The personality, education, personal skills, and drive to see this through to a profit.
5. The ability to assess and manage risk.

If you are unsure if buying a business is the right option for you, there are two others workbooks available in this same series. The first is called "Successfully Buy your Franchise: Expert advice from a Business Broker" or the second, "Successfully Start your Business: Expert advice from a Business Broker."

To help make the right decision about whether to buy an existing business, buy a franchise or start from scratch, consider the following:
Are you an Entrepreneur or an Intrapreneur?

My perception is that most main street or small business owners are either an entrepreneur or an intrapreneur. I see Entrepreneurs that own and run their own business and with the following characteristics:

✓ Highly independent
✓ Visionary
✓ Comfortable accepting higher risks
✓ Somewhat of a loner

I see Intrapreneurs that own and run their own business with the following characteristics:

✓ Tend to be more conservative
✓ Open to expert guidance
✓ Often more methodical, tending to mitigate risks
✓ Worked in corporate America; possibly in a management role and so understands reporting structures, accountability, project timelines, and working to achieve deadlines
✓ Tend to gravitate to the franchise business model as it provides structure and has systems already built and in place.

But how do I really know if business ownership is right for me?

From the research I've done and from my personal experience, I honestly don't think there is a black and white answer. I think the hardest part of deciding to pursue business ownership is actually making that decision, as you don't know the answer until you start.

My decision to move into business ownership came from the lack of alternatives. I looked at the managers I'd worked for and the people I knew in small business and concluded that I could do all they did and sometimes more. I then looked at people I knew in business ownership and decided I could match what they did if I paid attention to detail, sought opinions from those who were successful, and believed in myself. And I believe self-belief or self-confidence is a critical component of a successful business owner.

A few other thoughts.

A critical ingredient of successful business owners that I have been able to observe is a personality trait of being a positive thinker. Running and owning a business is not easy, especially if there are self doubts. Having a positive attitude that looks through those difficult times is a very important attribute.

Another critical thing I did was understand that business ownership came with risks. My success would be increased if I managed the risk of running a business by paying everyone when they were due, making sure the customer's expectations were exceeded, did my best to have happy and motivated employees, and paying attention to detail. All this sounds a bit simplistic but I've found it successful with the five businesses that I've owned.

Perhaps the final critical ingredient is having the support of those immediately around you such as your spouse and immediate family. Because they know who you are and understand you the best, they can support you when there are challenges running a business; and I am yet to talk to a business owner that hasn't experienced challenges. As they say, if it was easy, everyone would do it.

So how do you really know if business ownership is right for you? You don't. In the Aboriginal community of Australia they have a saying, No Dream, No Story, No Song. Dreaming is a critical part of Aboriginal life in Australia. The significance of dreaming is that it's used to inspire positive emotions to take action. The Aboriginal communities love telling stories. Because of their isolated environment and the fact they are nomadic meant that books were not part of their culture. However their culture is critical to them both individually and collectively. The way to educate their children and pass on their culture is through stories. The stories were about drought, flood, hunting, food, and survival in one of the most inhospitable places in the world. Finally, the other way of passing things on and remembering things is through song. Like a book, a song would be used to explain an historic event or even to give directions. Water is critical in the remote parts of Australia. If you don't have a book or a map, how do you give directions to food or water? You do it through a song that explains how to get from point A to point B and how long it all takes.

So the point of the above is that either you believe in yourself and believe in your dream of business ownership and go for it, or no dream, no story and no song.

Consider a SCORE counselor

Perhaps you would welcome talking to a SCORE counselor? SCORE is a non-profit organization that provides counseling services for potential or existing small business owners. They have local chapters throughout the United States where you can make an appointment with a counselor and get their advice for free on business ownership including operating, marketing, financial advice etc. They have a website at http://www.score.org where you can go to get more information and also easily navigate to their local chapter and phone or email to make an appointment to visit one of their counselors or advisors.

6 Personality Traits Of An Entrepreneur

This is an interesting topic in its own right but way beyond the scope of this workbook to address in too much depth. However, from the research I've done there seems to be agreement that the right personality traits may lead to a higher rate of success for would-be entrepreneurs. Here are some personality traits that have been suggested may be good to have if you want to be an entrepreneur.

1. *Natural intelligence*
   Being a genius is not essential. Similarly, too much education can be a hindrance. Limited or impacted intelligence will invariably provide failure.
2. *Strong leadership*
   This helps as the business develops not only by attracting people who want to work for the entrepreneur, but also assuring customers, suppliers and other business leaders related to the business.
3. *Hard work ethic*
   Almost without exception, successful businesses come from hard work.
4. *Independent thinkers*
   This is an interesting trait as it captures different things. For example, the ability to come up with an idea is part of it, but also the courage and ability to focus on where the business is going as opposed to being told by "experts" that it's going in the wrong direction.
5. *Street wise*
   This trait captures a few skills. These include the ability to think on their feet, understand hidden agenda, and when not to trust others.
6. *Motivation to succeed*
   This is probably one of the key ingredients for success. If you lack any of the above but this ingredient is high, then the chances of success are higher.

Some good news

The good news is that the following do not influence whether or not you will be successful as an entrepreneur. These traits are:

1. Age
2. Sex
3. Marriage
4. Education

Colonel Sanders was not deterred by his age of 62 in building one of the largest fried chicken businesses. Sex or gender is no longer an excuse; perhaps it could be argued that being a woman is in fact a plus. And as for education, we all know Bill Gates dropped out from Harvard during his sophomore year and Sir Winston Churchill never had an education higher than grade 3.

Final thought

If knowing whether or not you have the personal traits to be a successful entrepreneur are important to you, search the web for "Entrepreneur traits" or "Entrepreneur personality" etc. There are many articles on the topic but remember, whether or not you have the personal traits may be or may not be important but what is critical is being able to take action. No action = no result.

7 Stages Of The Business Life Cycle

After you buy your business and it becomes yours to make all ongoing decisions, it will be useful recognizing where your business is at, and how it fits in your local economy. If you are able to recognize what's happening, it will give you an insight about how your business is accepted and positioned, or more accurately, the product or service you are offering. Below are the 7 stages of a business life cycle. Be aware of these cycles as they will also influence many of the major decisions you make such as adding new hires, spending money on sales and marketing to grow the business, adding additional office or factory space to the business to grow it, to name a few examples.

1. Seed Stage:

The seed stage of your business life cycle is when your business is just a thought or an idea. This is the very conception or birth of a new business and where we are currently focused.
- ✓ Challenge: Most new businesses will have to overcome the initial challenge of market acceptance. A strategy for this situation would be to pursue one niche opportunity and be the best. That's where your business plan comes in as this will guide you. Do not spread money and time resources too thin.
- ✓ Focus: The focus for this stage of the business is on matching the business opportunity with your skills, experience, energy, and enthusiasm. Other focal points include deciding on a business ownership structure, finding professional advisors, and business planning.
- ✓ Money Sources: Early in the business life cycle with no proven market or customers, you will need to rely on your own cash or friends and family. Other potential sources include suppliers, customers, and government grants. Make sure you allocate time to uncover these funds.

2. Start-Up Stage:

Your business is born and now exists legally. Products or services are in production and you have your first customers.
- ✓ Challenge: If your business is in the start-up life cycle stage, it is likely you have overestimated money needs and the time to get to market. The main challenge is not to burn through what little cash you have. You need to learn what profitable needs your clients have and do a reality check to see if your business is on the right track.
- ✓ Focus: Start-ups require establishing a customer base and market presence along with tracking and conserving cash flow.
- ✓ Money Sources: Owner, friends, family, suppliers, customers, or grants.

3. Growth Stage:

Your business has made it through the toddler years and is now a child. Revenues and customers are increasing with many new opportunities and issues. Profits are strong, but competition is surfacing.
- ✓ Challenge: The biggest challenge for a growth company is dealing with the constant range of issues and their time and money demands. Strong management is required and a possible new business plan. Learn how to train and delegate to conquer this stage of development.
- ✓ Focus: Growth life cycle businesses are focused on running the business in a more formal way to deal with the increase in sales and customers. Better accounting and management systems need to be set-up. New employees will have to be hired to deal with the influx of business.
- ✓ Money Sources: Banks, profits, partnerships, grants, and leasing options.

4. Established Stage:

Your business has now matured into a thriving company with a place in the market and loyal customers. Sales growth is not explosive but manageable. Business life now becomes more routine.

- ✓ Challenge: It is far too easy to rest on your laurels during this life stage. You have worked hard and have earned a rest, but the marketplace is relentless and competitive. Stay focused on the bigger picture. Issues like the economy, competitors or changing customer tastes can quickly end all the hard work you've done.
- ✓ Focus: An established life cycle company will be focused on improvement and productivity. To compete in an established market, you will require better business practices along with automation and outsourcing to improve productivity.
- ✓ Money Sources: Profits, banks, investors, and government.

5. Expansion Stage:

This phase is characterized by a period of growth into new markets and distribution channels. This stage is often the choice of the small business owner to gain a larger market share and find new revenue and profit channels.
- ✓ Challenge: Moving into new markets requires the planning and research of a seed or start-up stage business. Focus should be on businesses that complement your existing experience and capabilities. Moving into unrelated businesses can be disastrous.
- ✓ Focus: Add new products or services to existing markets or expand existing business into new markets and customer types.
- ✓ Money Sources: Joint ventures, banks, licensing, new investors, and partners.

6. Decline Stage:

Changes in the economy, society, or market conditions can decrease sales and profits. This may quickly end many small companies.
- ✓ Challenge: Businesses in the decline stage of the life cycle will be challenged with dropping sales, profits, and negative cash flow. The biggest issue is how long the business can support a negative cash flow. Ask is it time to move on to the final life cycle stage...exit.
- ✓ Focus: Search for new opportunities and business ventures. Cutting costs and finding ways to sustain cash flow are vital for the declining stage.
- ✓ Money Sources: Suppliers, customers, owners.

7. Exit Stage:

This is the big opportunity for your business to cash out on all the effort and years of hard work. Or it can mean shutting down the business.
- ✓ Challenge: Selling a business requires your realistic evaluation. It may have been years of hard work to build the company, but what is its real value in the current market place?
- ✓ Focus: Get a proper valuation on your company. Look at your business operations, management and competitive barriers to make the company worth more to the buyer. Set-up legal buy-sell agreements along with a business transition plan.
- ✓ Money Sources: Find a business valuation partner. Consult with your accountant and financial advisors for the best tax strategy to sell or close down the business.

Each stage of the business life cycle may not occur in chronological order. Some businesses will be "built to flip", quickly going from start-up to exit. Others will choose to avoid expansion and stay in the established stage.

Whether your business is a glowing success or a dismal failure depends on your ability to adapt to its changing life cycles. What you focus on and overcome today will change in the future. Understanding where your business fits in the business life cycle will help you foresee upcoming challenges and make the best decisions. This may include accepting an offer should the right buyer come along.

Expectations: Seller Vs Buyer

The following may be interesting as you move through your business buying processes. I'm sure you will have many thoughts and discussions about the seriousness of the seller or another party you are working with and sometimes become a little frustrated. We all tend to see things through our own eyes so the purpose of the following is simply to suggest there may be another perspective from the one you are seeing. Having the ability to accept there is another perspective may in fact determine whether you are successful or not at buying a business.

The seller expects to:

1. Receive all cash up front;
2. Provide one week of training;
3. Provide the buyer with one day to do their due diligence;
4. Close the offer the day after the completion of due diligence;
5. Be paid five to six times the business earnings or discretionary earnings.

The buyer expects to:

1. Buy a business with 10% down payment;
2. Receive two months of training free of charge from the seller;
3. Have four weeks to complete their due diligence;
4. Work in the business for 30 days to "test drive" it;
5. Pay no more than one year's worth of business earnings or discretionary earnings.

About where the seller and the buyer meet:

1. The down payment from the buyer is about equal to the business earnings or discretionary earnings;
2. Seller provides some financing;
3. Seller provides two to three weeks of training;
4. Buyer receives two weeks to complete their due diligence;
5. It takes 45 to 60 days to close;
6. The business is sold between two to three times earnings.

7 "Musts" Before Buying Your Business

You have decided to buy your own business and obviously want to get it right. Your first thought is to talk to a few people in business ownership to see if they have some suggestions. Your next thought is to start reading some books and magazines and reading newspaper articles you previously didn't take any interest in. You start watching what they do at the businesses you go to and feel pretty sure this is something you can do. And you are right. This is something you can do. There are many variables to consider; practical issues such as what, where, how, and when with legal, financial, management, operational, and marketing questions. Then there are the emotional considerations with the highs and lows of getting started and sometimes being confused and overwhelmed.

Let's take a breath! What can we do to make our decision to buy a business successful and with as little pain as possible?

Must # 1:

Be patient with yourself. You can make buying a business overwhelming, just like anything else we do in life. Be comfortable that there is a lot to learn but it can be learned and what you need to know is finite. To help you, there are resources available such as SCORE, Small Business Development Centers, websites online you can easily find with a Google search using a key word, magazines such as Inc and Success, newspapers such as the Wall Street Journal as well as the business section of your local paper, and a wide range of professionals.

Must # 2:

One of the most important things you need to do is find your Buyer Profile. Your buyer profile requires you to look inside yourself to know the industry, business type, your business background and experience, what you enjoy doing and don't enjoy doing, your professional skill set etc so you focus your energy on finding a business that matches your profile rather than looking at opportunities that don't and then burning out from the process. In Section Three we look deeper into your Buyer Profile to help you uncover where you need to focus.

Must # 3:

Use your gift! Before you look at all the different businesses to buy, see what you do easily and naturally to see if this can be the basis of your business. For example, if you were a dancer as a child can this be the basis of your business? Some options could include starting a dance studio for children, open a retail store that sells children's dance clothes, open a book store that sells dancing books, magazines, photos etc. Perhaps you had a gift for singing. Consider a business that coaches people to sing, a retail store that sells musical instruments, a weekly newspaper that specializes in promoting singers, a website that sells records or material of specific singers etc. Reawaken your gift and see if you can buy an existing business and add your gift to the product range so it takes that business to the next level.

Must # 4:

This is my favorite. You've decided to buy a business so I would recommend you look at putting a plan together. If you fail to plan, you plan to fail. Buying a business is a great idea but it needs to be accompanied by a plan. Although the planning process may seem unnecessary and tedious, it will benefit you in the future. For example, when you need to talk with an attorney about legal questions or an accountant about financial statements or to the bank to borrow some money, you need some structure dealing with these issues. Plus you can use the template of a business plan to keep you focused, show where you are and more importantly, where you are going. Your business plan should be a work in progress and constantly changes. If you want more information about using a business plan, please go to Section Seven.

Must # 5:

Recognize that when you buy your business one of your scarcest resources will be money. Therefore, the scarce amount of money you have must be spent wisely. Things can quickly eat up your limited capital so creating a budget and sticking to it, is important. Further in this section there is a start up expense planner, while in Section Three there is a Personal Budget planner. My recommendation is that if you are planning on buying a business, consider cutting back some of your current personal expenditure in preparation for business ownership. The discipline will hold you in good stead and will be one less adjustment.

Must # 6:

Buying a business comes with challenges. Find a way to motivate yourself and stay motivated! One of the best ways to do that is by using a Productivity Plan. This is talked about more in Section Seven but a Productivity Plan is a simple "To do" list of things you want done. This can be a great motivator as you can look back after two weeks and review what you did and see how much you've done since. You may make mistakes, but how else do you learn? The challenge is to keep going so the tide of success flows with you.

Must # 7:

Patience is a virtue - another great maxim we've all heard, but critically important if you are buying a business for the first time. Be confident, be determined, be energetic, but above all be patient.

Buying a business has many challenges. It comes with uncertainty, lack of a support structure, no road map, and probably against our natural tendencies to look for reassuring guideposts. Plus, the uncertainties are there to guide you. However, the professional and personal rewards greatly outweigh the sacrifices, plus the things we learn allow us to be stronger and financially secure for the next steps of our journey.

No Dream, No Story, No Song – 8 Dream Killers

Business ownership is not for everyone. No question about it. One of my main goals in writing this guide is to provide as much information as possible in as logical order as possible so you, and only you can make that final decision about whether you will buy an existing business and become a business owner. I'm sure you have read or heard before that someone once observed: "Everyone is an expert in at least two areas: telling you how to raise *your* kids and telling you how to lead *your* life." My children tell me that all the time. Perhaps there should be a third area: "others telling you how to run *your* business." Everyone loves to think they are helping - it's only human nature. Everyone has an opinion and we like nothing better than sharing their opinion – be it valuable or not. Because it's delivered with such good intention, when we don't follow the advice we feel bad. Perhaps the hardest advice we get are the "horror" stories from people who are close to us. If you are thinking about buying a business it will be a difficult decision and you will get naysayers. However, the bottom line is that it's your life, you get to make the final decision…and that's the way it should be.

So here are eight reasons you can use **not** to start your own business. Incidentally, I have explained why the eight reasons are not valid but once again, in the end you get to make that final decision – that's what following your dream is all about.

1. A 'loved one' or spouse dream killer:

This is probably the most important of them all. The business buyer talks it over with his loved one or significant other and thinks they have agreement they will start a new business. When the decision day comes the agreement is not as forthcoming as first thought as objections and concerns begin to flow.

Answer: Starting and owning a business must be a *joint decision*. Business ownership will impact your family in a way that a having a job change doesn't. If it's scary for you, imagine how it must feel to those around you. They have less information about what you are thinking of doing or they may not be as informed. Even before the search begins, a married couple needs frank, honest discussions about the benefits and problems of business ownership.

2. The "Passion" dream killer:

Often you will hear or read that you must have a "passion" for your product or service. And if you don't have that passion, don't get involved. How much passion can you maintain doing the same thing day in and day out?

Answer: There are two important points. Firstly, you are running a business and it's your responsibility as the owner to run it correctly by following the appropriate laws, ensuring customer service is as high as possible, all the bills are paid etc. If you don't run the business properly then everything goes away. Secondly, the "passion" you need is building a viable and ongoing business so you can feed and maintain you and/or your family and then make some money when you sell your business. *Passion for building a business is also a great passion to have* and it well may be that the product or service is just incidental in that case.

3. The friend or neighbor dream killer:

Not only does everyone love to be asked for their advice but even more they love to give it. When you buy a new car or get a job promotion or have big news we love to share it with friends and neighbors, that's why they are family and friends. Unfortunately telling others what we do seems to automatically provide the right to give their advice even if they do not know anything about the subject. I'm always ready to give my opinion on anything! Just ask!

Answer: Without being rude or close minded, try to limit the input from well meaning, but non-expert people. If you are serious about starting you new business there may be value in not discussing it with some family or friends simply because you do not want to be burdened with the uninformed opinions of others.

4. The "been there – done that" dream killer:

This one's real simple. You are certain to know family, friends or work colleagues who considered business ownership and for whatever reason they decided not to move forward with it. So when they hear of your plans to start a new business they like nothing more than explaining in great detail why you shouldn't.

Answer: Focus on YOUR goals, and tune out uninformed or ill-reasoned advice, whatever the source. It does not matter whether the person who is trying to hold you back is doing it for the right reasons or not. All that matters is if the advice is accurate and solid. If it is, then pay attention to it.

5. The "cold feet" dream killer:

This is probably the most common dream killer, and unfortunately, is self-inflicted as we do it to ourselves. Starting a business is probably one of the three biggest decisions we make in life next to choosing a spouse and buying your first house. If you have a spouse or have at least bought one home you can remember the thought you gave and how it was a little bit scary. Deciding to go into business is a big thing, and it is definitely scary. So what can happen is that we set up a way to avoid that hard and scary decision by finding reasons to justify *not* going into business. We allow our fears to get ahead of our hopes. We deprive ourselves of the opportunity to achieve the very thing we most want...the independence, security and freedom that comes with being the boss of a successful business.

Answer: We must embrace being scared and use the fear factor to our advantage by letting it add an extra element of caution and care to our research. After you have clearly set your goals through your business plan, you must compare several different opportunities to each other to see which one most closely matches your "perfect business model."

6. The "sample of one" dream killer:

Too often potential business owners get feedback from one person about a particular business and make all future decisions on that one piece of feedback. Advice from just one person is always dangerous, and unfortunately this one works in both directions. For example, you may talk with someone who failed in that business or worse yet, just in the particular industry. As a result the potential business owner concludes the business is not for them - a rash conclusion. And conversely, the potential business owner hears one single success story and decides this is the business for them. Another rash conclusion!

Answer: A "sample of one" is always dangerous as it is too general. Also, it should not be attempted until you have a solid core of data collected over time from many reliable sources. Bottom line; check multiple opinions from multiple sources and take care to ask the same questions the same way so you get a complete picture. Don't ask multiple people a different set of questions as you have no true basis for comparison whether your final decision is positive or negative about the business, and whether it is a good "fit".

7. The "wrong set of questions" dream killer:

Often new business owners destroy their own dreams of business ownership by confusing casual inquiry with real research. For example, you may be considering a retail business and may try to find how many similar businesses are listed in the Yellow Pages. That's an interesting idea but it doesn't indicate the real size of that market. If it's a business in a niche market, you need to understand the proximity of each business. It may well be the market in that area is under-served!

Answer: You must do your own research about the national, regional and local economy, the industry, and the specific business you're planning to start. This is probably the hardest part for a new business owner starting out. You need to speak to as many of them as you can, to get as many opinions as you can. If you can find a similar business in another location, speak to the owner to see if they are willing to share ideas with you. It may be, if you are not a direct competitive threat, that you could work together, share business plans and sales and marketing ideas, buy collectively and thereby get better wholesale prices, build employee manuals, and training manuals etc.

8. Paralysis by analysis:

Another form of dream killer, this describes people who never make a decision because their research never ends. Clear and detailed personal due diligence on any business opportunity is a must. Seek out *qualified* advice, but make sure it's qualified. Of course, talk to others in the same type of business that you are contemplating. Seek out attorneys, CPA's, and other qualified business experts but stay away from "expert opinions" from people who are not experts. There comes a time, however, when you have done enough research. It is time to make up your mind and make a decision. Acknowledge that research cannot answer every question. Some questions cannot be answered until you actually commit to a business, start doing it and then learn what the market has to tell you.

Answer: Clearly focus on your goals as you built them in your business plan and researched them and have faith in your own judgment. These are the best tools to avoid the indecision that comes from over-analysis.

Conclusion:

After you have done them all, review the data, and ask yourself these questions:
1. Do I still want to go into business for myself?
2. Have I discovered what it takes to be successful in this business, in terms of others who have already done this business, and in terms of opportunity in my marketplace?
   a. If so, do I fit the business?
   b. Am I like the people who have already succeeded in it?
   c. Do I know what the successful owner does?
   d. Can I do, or learn to do, what the successful owner does?
   e. Do I want to do what the successful owner does?
3. Assuming I succeed in this business, will it allow me to reach the personal, professional, and family goals that I need from my business?
4. Is this the best business I have found to help me achieve my goals?

If the answer to all the above questions is "yes," then move forward with your goal of starting your business. If the answer to even a single one is "no," then it is not the business for you. Only if the answer is "I don't know," should you do more research. Knowledge of yourself, your goals, and your priorities is critical to making a good decision.

Passion - Good Or Bad?

As a business broker I keep hearing buyers or new business owners starting out reacting to something they have been told by family or well-meaning friends, and this is, if they intend going into business ownership make sure you: "Find your passion!" Focus on what you're passionate about and your likelihood of success increases.

I have thought a lot about "passion" and here's what I've come up with: After a short period of time the passion we had for something starts to slide. We need to look no further for this than our spouse or significant other or even our immediate family and friends. To re-invigorate these critical relationships that sustain us through life we celebrate birthdays, anniversaries, and special occasions such as Thanksgiving and Christmas, other important events such as Easter or July 4th plus ones that are important to us individually such as graduation from college etc.

So this lack of passion we often experience in life with the job we have been doing leads us to think "There must be more." That is when we start to think "Let me start a business of my own and do it my way."

Roadblock or Reality?

If that's the place in life where you are at, my advice to you would be "don't dwell on passion or it will become a roadblock for you." And here's why. There are so many different types of businesses you can start. In the end your decision will boil down to three main things which all come together in one final question. The three things are:
1) How much money do you have to invest to start your business?
2) What lifestyle do you want this business to create for you?
3) Do you have the self-belief that you have the skill to be successful?

If your answers to all three are yes then your final question will be: When I weigh these three things together, do I feel ready to take the financial AND emotional risk? Taking the financial risk is both an emotional and logical decision however taking the emotional risk is probably the hardest because there is no logic to it. Questions race through your mind such as "What will I do if I fail? What will I tell my family and friends if I fail? What will I do next? What will I tell the employees or …? How will I recover from that lost money? How will I repay any debts I may have?

So passion's nice, but it's not critical. Consider some current business owners. There is the restaurant owner who has to multi-task with food, employees, customers, and a landlord. There is the hair salon owner who has to multi-task with the different hair styles, employees, customers, and landlord. There is the auto mechanic who has to multi-task with the different make and models of cars, employees, customers, and landlord.

I'm sure you get the point. Again, passion is good but not what this is all about. It's all about living your life with passion with your family, friends and things that are important to you (lifestyle), by finding the right business that will provide the means for you to do that.

Passion is more about what you are being (**business owner**), than it is about what you are doing.

End Of Chapter Notes

Use this page to write down notes, ideas and other brainstorming for buying your business.

Section Two

Education

"*Be curious always! For knowledge will not acquire you: you must acquire it.*"

Dr. John G. Hibben

Introduction

The purpose of Section Two is to introduce some of the core and peripheral topics all business owners need to deal with when buying their business. To put some logic to the order, the first topics cover legal subjects you need to be aware of. I am not an attorney so if you need specific information, make sure you contact an attorney who can help you. The next subject is general business needs such as insurance and then a focus on some basic financial tools and concepts that are useful to know as a business owner. To help you with the financial tools, I have loaded onto my website sample Excel and Word documents you can download and use. The next topics cover finance options which will help if you need to borrow from a third party lender to buy your business followed by an overview of the main documents you will find in a business transaction. This section then concludes with a look at the process used in valuing a business, plus the different types of professionals you can hire to help you buy your business.

Business ownership is an exciting world. There is always something new to learn, a problem to address, constant personal and professional growth, meeting new and different people from different walks of life and the stimulation of being a business owner, making your own decisions, and having fun. If you have questions about any of the material covered in this section, please send me an email to info@andrew-rogerson.com

---

The Perfect Business

Once you buy your business, make all your decisions on the basis that it is always for sale. This will drive the disciplines you need to be successful. Also, if you find an interested buyer your business and you are ready to go.

The perfect business is one with the following attributes:

1. A reasonable price
2. A reasonable down payment (hopefully about 30% of the full price)
3. Some seller financing
4. Reasonable sales (hopefully increasing each year)
5. Discretionary earnings of $60,000 per annum or more
6. A compelling reason for sale
7. A desired industry type
8. Good and attractive location (if important for the business type)

Legal Entity Options

Once you complete negotiations to buy your business, you will move into Due Diligence, examine the claims of the seller, close due diligence to open escrow and then close escrow to now be the new owner of the business. Just prior to or just after closing escrow, an important decision to make is the best form of legal entity. Your final decision does not mean you cannot change your mind or move from one entity to the other at a later stage. However, if you change entity it will incur costs from working directly with your accountant and/or attorney as well as any government filing fees.

If you want to file your own legal entity, you can do this yourself but if you want the right advice and the best information for your specific situation at a minimum, consult with an attorney, and if you are concerned about tax consequences, first consult with your accountant.

The following is a brief overview of the different legal entities:

Sole Proprietor

As a sole proprietor you will be responsible for all liabilities and debts in a business, so this is your legal exposure as the law views a sole proprietor and the business essentially as one and the same. You will also receive the profits and assets generated by the business so this is your financial exposure. A sole proprietor is the simplest type of business entity with all profits reported as personal income and taxed at your personal tax rates so this is your tax exposure. This can be a disadvantage once the business gets established and starts to generate a high level of profit and where you will need the services of a good accountant or tax agent. And remember, profit does not equal cash flow. You can be making a lot of money that attracts high taxes but be cash poor because all your profits are sitting in your business as accounts receivable.

The good news for using a Sole Proprietor as your legal entity is that there are no filing fees to either the Federal or State governments.

Partnership

A common way to spread risk, bring together two or more like-minded people, or create an entity that allows a number of people to come together with complementary skill sets and/or interests, is through a partnership. As partners you share ownership of a business by spreading around the downside or risks, based on each person's capital infusions. You also share the upside which is the profits of the business or its gain when the business is sold. To protect all partners in the business, you need to have a legal agreement drafted that defines the division of profits and assets, how much each partner will contribute in capital, how disputes will be resolved, provisions for adding additional partners, and how the business should be dissolved or bought out by a partner.

A legal agreement is important because, like any relationship, not all business partners are good matches and the situation could eventually change. Similar to Sole Proprietors, partners and the business itself are viewed as one entity by the law. There are three types of partnerships:

General Partnership: A joint venture that is typically shared equally (unless otherwise stated in the legal agreement), with equal division of profits, losses and responsibilities.

Limited Partnership: This form of partnership generally specifies that the participants have limited liability and also limits the input to management decisions. This structure may not work well for service or retail businesses and is best used for bringing in investors for short term projects.

Joint Venture: This structure is used for a short term investment or project. If the partners continue working together on an ongoing basis, the structure must be changed to one of the other options.

Final thought

Is a partnership a good business option? The honest answer is that it is a good business option but that it has the highest probability of not working out. A lot of businesses close down for different reasons and these can include partner disputes, frustration at not being able to achieve what brought the partners together in the first place, or the partners not realizing that they thought they were just bringing a partner into the business, not his spouse and children, who have their own demands and dynamic.

Corporation

Corporations came into existence to provide legal protection for the owners of the business and to allow an interest in the business to be sold in exchange for an investor putting in capital that generated a return on that investment. An interest in the business is also known as a share. A corporation is its own entity that is taxed, can be sued, and can enter into contractual agreements in its own right. The owners of a corporation are shareholders who elect a board of directors to oversee the major decisions and policies of the company. Since the corporation is its own entity, it can continue even when ownership changes hands. Shareholders in corporations have less liability than sole proprietors, however, officers of the company can be held liable for legal matters such as failing to pay taxes or payroll. Corporations can deduct the cost of benefits for employees, officers, and as we said above, can raise capital by selling shares of the company stock.

Incorporating requires a significant amount of paperwork and corporations must comply with federal, state, and some local agencies. Dividends that are paid to shareholders are not deductible as business income, which can result in paying higher taxes. This is also known as a C Corporation.

Creating a corporation is usually done in your home state but you can incorporate in another US state that doesn't have fees nor tax the profits of out-of-state income, also called a foreign corporation. Keep in mind, if you do incorporate somewhere other than your home state, you may have to pay additional fees and meet additional requirements. For the full understanding of all the options, you may want to speak with an accountant or tax advisor before making a final decision.

Because Corporations are an effective legal and tax entity, it was decided to make this option available to individuals including families and this is known as the S Corp.

Subchapter "S" Corporation

This is a tax election that allows a shareholder to treat profits as distributions and pass through to his or her personal tax return. This means that the shareholder must be paid a salary that meets the standards of "reasonable compensation" – meaning that the wages are comparable to what would be paid to someone in a similar position. If this is not done, the IRS can reclassify the business and require the shareholder to pay taxes on all of the profits and earnings.

Limited Liability Company (LLC)

A Limited Liability Company is a relatively new structure that bridges the gap between a general partnership and a corporation, bringing together the protection from personal liability offered by corporations, and the flexibility of a partnership. The duration of a LLC is determined when the business is filed, though it can be extended if members agree. LLC's must not have more than two of the four characteristics that define corporations: limited liability to the extent of assets; continuity of life; centralization of management; and free transferability of ownership interests. Federal tax forms for LLC's are typically the same as the forms used for partnerships. However, if more than two of the characteristics that define a corporation exist, the business must file corporation forms.

Given the complexities, legal, and tax ramifications and benefits of each business structure, it is important to consult with your accountant and/or attorney to get the best advice on your particular situation.

If you would like to do some additional research before meeting with your accountant or attorney, go the IRS website at www.irs.gov

Federal Income Tax:

The method of paying federal income tax depends on your legal form of business. The following apply for the different entities:

Sole Proprietorship:

Federal income tax for a Sole Proprietor is made with your Schedule C tax return and part of your Form 1040 Federal Income Tax return.

Partnership:

A Federal Partnership return is filed or Form 1065. This is an informational return that shows gross and net earnings of profit and loss which flows to the individuals earnings of each partner when they complete and report their individual return on Form 1040.

Corporation:

Corporations must file an 1120 tax return for the entity in its own right. Any earnings from the corporation including salary and other income such as dividends are then reported on your personal federal individual return on Form 1040.

Federal Payroll Tax:

If a business employs a person they must register with the IRS and acquire an Employer Identification Number and pay federal withholding tax at least quarterly.

Fictitious Business Name Or DBA

Once you have decided on your legal entity it may be necessary to create a Fictitious Business Name or Doing Business As (DBA). If the current owner of the business has a DBA, this is something you will definitely want as part of your decision to buy the business unless you plan on renaming the business. If you plan to rename the business I would recommend against this unless there is a significant reason to do this. Part of your purchase of the existing business will be goodwill and that goodwill includes the current business name. Changing the business name can reduce the value of that goodwill, so be careful.

If you intend to use the current DBA of the business as part of your purchase, you will want to have legal ownership of the DBA. It will therefore be necessary for the seller to abandon the DBA and you come in directly behind the seller's action and register the DBA. DBA's are handled at a County level, so check with your County on the process to follow.

If you've decided to create a new DBA or Fictitious Business Name, the new name will require filing with the local county and it depends on the legal entity you have chosen. For example, if you have decided to operate as a sole proprietor the only name you can really use when you market yourself is your name. This may not suit you as you may want to sound like a large company or your personal name doesn't reflect the service you provide. For example, if your business is cutting hair and your name is Bill Smith, that doesn't sound like a good business name to use. Hair Cuts for All or $10 Hair Cuts or Elite Hair Salon has much more appeal.

Conversely, you may have chosen to incorporate, and plan on having multiple locations with different names, for example, a series of bars. One name could be Sacramento Bar and Grill, one could be Reno Bar and Grill and one could be New York's Finest Bar and Grille. Guess where they are located?

In some U.S. states you register your assumed name with the Secretary of State or other state agency, but in most states, registration is handled at the county level, and each county may have different forms and fees for registering a name. Generally speaking, the process is fairly simple: you perform a search through their database to make sure the name is not already in use, then submit a simple form, along with the correct filing fee (anywhere from $10 to $50). Some states also require that you publish a notice in your local newspaper and submit an affidavit to show that you have fulfilled the publication requirement. Call your county clerk's office to find out the local fees and procedures in your area.

Use the template below to brainstorm some business names that reflect the image and character of the business you are going to open.

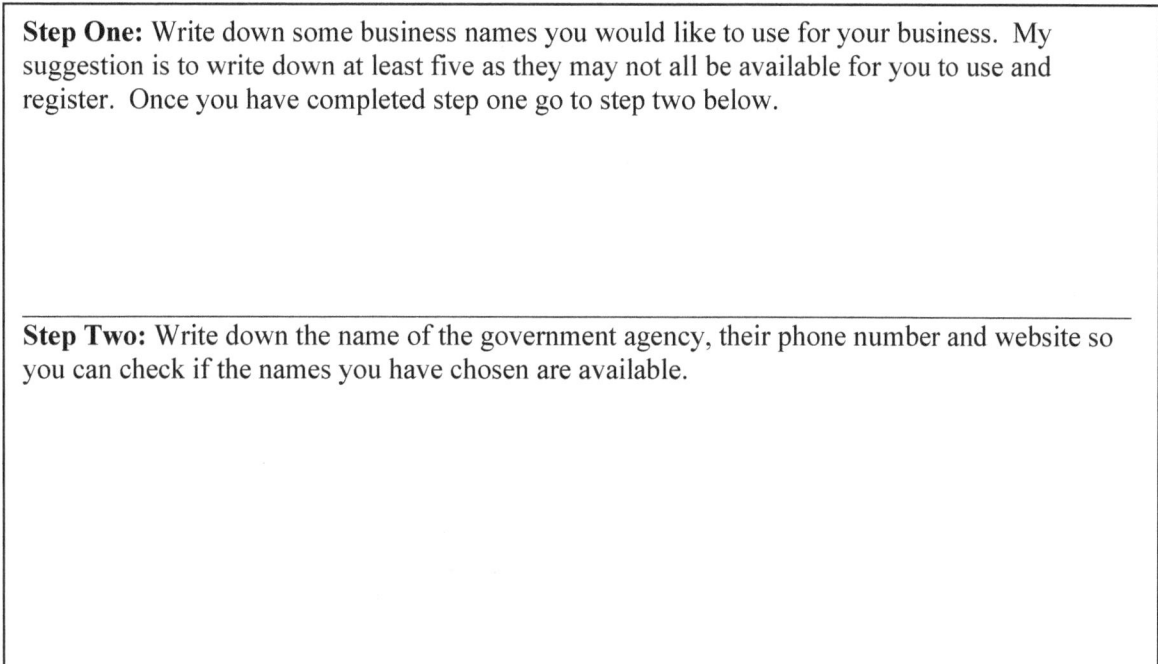

Step One: Write down some business names you would like to use for your business. My suggestion is to write down at least five as they may not all be available for you to use and register. Once you have completed step one go to step two below.

Step Two: Write down the name of the government agency, their phone number and website so you can check if the names you have chosen are available.

Federal Employer Identification Number

Each business operating in the United States needs a valid Employer Identification Number (EIN). It's like a Social Security Number for a business and is used for tax reporting purposes. An EIN is required if you have one or more employees on a payroll, or if you have chosen to create a corporation or partnership. If your business has started its life as a sole proprietorship and you don't do certain types of business activities you are not required to apply for an EIN. However, if you are concerned about sending your Social Security number to businesses asking for your EIN, you can apply for an EIN to the IRS.

For more information about EIN's and lots of other good business information, go to the IRS website http://www.irs.gov and work your way down through the Businesses tab or do a search for what you need. I did not include URL's to specific sites within the IRS as the pages may get updated or changed and thereby superseding the URL.

Another excellent site for business information is the US government site: http://www.business.gov

Business License And Other Licenses And Permits

Every state, city, and county has different regulations for general business licenses. A business license allows you to comply with your area business requirements. The fees range from $50 to $300 and are renewed each year.

Certain types of businesses may also be required to apply for special business licenses. For example, businesses dealing with alcoholic beverages, firearms, used goods or adult entertainment may require special license approval. Some businesses may require a permit issued by the local sheriff or other enforcement agency. Make sure you are aware of these requirements as you may have to pay a fine or in the worst case, close down and be prohibited from opening again. These licenses can also take longer to be issued, sometimes up to three months, so be sure to apply early.

The other license to be aware of is a Contractor's License. A lot of states regulate the minimum education and experience standards for contractors to perform work. In California, all regulations are the responsibility of the Contractors State License Board. Check your state government to see if you have similar requirements if you are planning on starting your business in one of these industries. The websites below may be able to assist you.

Business License Resources by State

- ✓ Alabama – www.ador.state.al.us/licenses/authrity/html
- ✓ Alaska – www.dced.state.ak.us/occ/buslic.htm
- ✓ Arizona – www.revenue.state.az.us/license.htm
- ✓ Arkansas – www.state.ar.us/online_business.php
- ✓ California – www.calgold.ca.gov/
- ✓ Colorado – www.state.co.us/gov_dir/obd/blid.htm
- ✓ Connecticut – www.state.ct.us/
- ✓ Delaware – www.state.de.us/revenue/obt/obtmain.htm
- ✓ District of Columbia – www.dcra.dc.gov/
- ✓ Florida – http://sun6.dms.state.fl.us/dor/businesses/
- ✓ Georgia – www.sos.state.ga.us/corporations/regforms.htm
- ✓ Hawaii – www.hawaii.gov/dbedt/start/starting.html
- ✓ Idaho – www.idoc.state.id.us/Pages/BUSINESSPAGE.html
- ✓ Illinois – www.sos.state.il.us/departments/business_services/business.html
- ✓ Indiana – www.state.in.us/sic/owners/ia.html
- ✓ Iowa – www.iowasmart.com/blic/
- ✓ Kansas – www.accesskansas.org/businesscenter/index.html?link=start
- ✓ Kentucky – www.thinkkentucky.com/kyedc/ebpermits.asp
- ✓ Louisiana – www.sec.state.la.us/comm/fss/fss-index.htm
- ✓ Maine – www.econdevmaine.com/biz-develop.htm
- ✓ Maryland – www.dllr.state.md.us/
- ✓ Massachusetts – www.state.ma.us/sec/cor/coridx.htm
- ✓ Michigan – http://medc.michigan.org/services/startups/index2.asp
- ✓ Minnesota – www.dted.state.mn.uss
- ✓ Mississippi – www.olemiss.edu/depts/mssbdc/going_intobus.html
- ✓ Missouri – www.ded.state.mo.us/business/businesscenter/
- ✓ Montana – www.state.mt.us/sos/biz/htm
- ✓ Nebraska – www.nebraska.gov/business/html/337/index.phtml
- ✓ New Hampshire – www.nhsbdc.org/startup.htm

- ✓ New Jersey – www.state.nj.us/njbiz/s_lic_and_cert.shtml
- ✓ New Mexico – http://edd.state.nm.us/NMBUSINESS/
- ✓ Nevada – www.nv.gov
- ✓ North Carolina – www.secstate.state.nc.us/secstate/blio/default.htm
- ✓ North Dakota – www.state.nd.us/sec/
- ✓ Ohio – www.state.oh.us/sos/business_services_information.htm
- ✓ Oklahoma – www.okonestop.com/
- ✓ Oregon – www.filinginoregon.com
- ✓ Pennsylvania – www.paopenforbusiness.state.pa.us
- ✓ Rhode Island – www.corps.state.ri.us/firststop/index.asp
- ✓ South Carolina – www.state.sd.us/STATE/sitecategory.cfm?mp=Licenses/Occupations
- ✓ South Dakota - www.sd.gov/Main_Login.asp
- ✓ Tennessee – www.state.tn.us/ecd/res_guide.htm
- ✓ Texas – www.tded.state.tx.us/guide/
- ✓ Utah – www.commerce.state.ut.us/web/commerce/admin/licen.htm
- ✓ Vermont – www.sec.state.vt.us/
- ✓ Virginia – www.dba.state.va.us/
- ✓ Washington – www.wa.gov/dol/bpd/limsnet.htm
- ✓ West Virginia – www.state.wv.us/taxrev//busreg.html
- ✓ Wisconsin – www.wdfi.org/corporations/forms/
- ✓ Wyoming – http://soswy.state.wy.us/corporat/corporat.htm

NOTE: Please be aware these weblinks may change as the website is updated. If this specific URL does not work, please go to the main Home Page of the website and do a search to find what you are looking for.

Additional Resources:
- ✓ The IRS also offers links to every state with multiple business resources:
  www.irs.gov/businesses/small/article/0,,id=99021,00.html

- ✓ Business.gov provides legal and regulatory information to small businesses in the U.S. This site is loaded with excellent information for every state to help entrepreneurs find answers and resolve problems and can be found at:
  www.Business.gov.

Sales And Use Taxes

At a national level there is currently no sales tax levied or paid on any goods and services. However, at a state level this sort of tax does apply except for the states of Alaska, Delaware, Montana, New Hampshire, and Oregon. If your business sells taxable goods and you are in a state in the US that collects sales tax, you will need to apply for a resale license. A resale license or Sales Tax Exemption Certificate will be needed if you purchase from wholesalers, allowing you to buy your merchandise without paying sales tax. This also means that you are responsible for collecting taxes when you make a sale. Each state and local authority has different requirements for tax rates, collection, and reporting methods. The Business Owner's Tool Kit website has an excellent directory of tax requirements for each state: www.toolkit.cch.com/text/P07_4500.asp

Insurance Options

When the subject of insurance comes up we tend to want to run and hide as it's something we hope we don't need. Plus it can get pretty complicated trying to understand all the variables, decide your risk comfort, and when it's all said and done, how much you can afford to pay. Hence there are different insurance policies for different reasons. The main policies you may wish to consider when you buy your business are below. However, as you explore the different insurance options, the insurance companies you contact will be glad to advise you on what you are inquiring about and make suggestions.

Use the templates at the end of this topic to do some comparison shopping and get this task accomplished. It may also be worth doing a little research now rather than wait until you are about to close escrow on your business and move into the training and day to day operations.

Liability Insurance or General Business Insurance

General Business Insurance or Liability Insurance protects you from lawsuits filed for accidents, injuries and negligence. Also, under this policy, if you are ever the target of a frivolous lawsuit, your insurance policy should take care of the legal fees and litigations. Not all policies are created equal, however, so be sure to check the details of any policy that you consider. Also, if you are going to lease a commercial location for your business, your landlord will probably require proof of liability insurance. Since the premiums can vary, it is a good idea to get some quotes early on and build this expense into your budget.

Business Interruption

If your business ceases to operate due to a fire or some other form of accident there are taxes, utilities and other continuing expenses to pay until the building is rebuilt and you can recommence trading. Business Interruption insurance provides money to pay fixed expenses until you are operational again.

Commercial Property Insurance

In the event of a disaster from fire, smoke, hail or wind the commercial property could be damaged. Coverage also extends to vandalism and civil disobedience. If you are renting the building, the property owner probably carries some level of insurance. You should ask what is covered in their policy. When in doubt, it is always best to carry your own policy.

Worker's Compensation Insurance

Many states now require that companies with employees carry worker's compensation insurance. This type of policy covers damages resulting from employee injuries. It is relatively expensive in some states (like California) so it would be wise to factor this into your plan early. Check the state listings provided in this chapter to find out if your area requires that you carry worker's comp insurance.

Commercial Auto Insurance

If you have a company vehicle or a business that makes deliveries, you will need a commercial auto policy. These policies can include coverage for collisions, comprehensive, rental cars, and towing. Also check your existing coverage of vehicles for both you and your employees (if applicable), since personal auto insurance does not always cover claims that occur during business operation.

Professional Liability Insurance

If your business is providing services, you should consider having professional liability insurance (also known as errors and omissions insurance). This type of liability coverage protects your business against malpractice, errors, and negligence in provision of services to your customers. Depending on your profession, you may be required by your state government to carry such a policy. For example, physicians are required to purchase malpractice insurance as a condition of practicing in certain states.

Life Insurance

If you are the main bread winner in your family or you have debts that need to be paid, then life insurance is the means to protect your loved ones. With a good life insurance policy, if you should be accidentally killed then the insurance policy will pay off both your personal and business debts if the correct amount of coverage is in place. Check into this one thoroughly as debt can cripple a family and for a relatively small monthly premium provide a lot of peace and mind. Also, if you intend getting an SBA loan to buy your business, you will need a policy to include cover that repays the value of your SBA loan in full on your death. Plus you may want additional coverage to leave for your spouse and family.

Key Man Insurance

This policy is complementary to Life Insurance mentioned above. If you (and/or any other individual) are so critical to the operation of your business that it cannot continue in the event of your illness or death, you should consider "key man" insurance. This type of policy is frequently required by banks or government loan programs. It also can be used to provide continuity in operations during a period of ownership transition caused by the death or incapacitation of an owner or other "key" employee.

Officer and Director

Under most state laws, officers and directors of a corporation may become personally liable for their actions on behalf of the company. This type of policy covers this liability.

Home-Based Business Insurance

Contrary to popular belief, homeowners' insurance policies do not generally cover home-based business losses. Depending on risks to your business, you may add riders to your homeowners' policy to cover normal business risks such as property damage. However, homeowner's policies only go so far and you may need to buy additional cover for other risks, such as general and professional liability.

Where to Locate Insurance Providers

Contact the broker that handles your auto or home owner's insurance to find out if he also offers business insurance. If not, they should be able to refer you to someone who does. You can also visit www.InsuranceFinder.com for a list of resources by state or Google the web.

To help evaluate different policies from different insurance companies, the following may help.

Insurance company name:	
Name of Agent:	
Contact number:	
Coverage key points including amount	
Premium quoted:	
Notes:	

Insurance company name:	
Name of Agent:	
Contact number:	
Coverage key points including amount	
Premium quoted:	
Notes:	

Insurance company name:	
Name of Agent:	
Contact number:	
Coverage key points including amount	
Premium quoted:	
Notes:	

Insurance company name:	
Name of Agent:	
Contact number:	
Coverage key points including amount	
Premium quoted:	
Notes:	

Insurance company name:	
Name of Agent:	
Contact number:	
Coverage key points including amount	
Premium quoted:	
Notes:	

Insurance company name:	
Name of Agent:	
Contact number:	
Coverage key points including amount	
Premium quoted:	
Notes:	

Patents/Trademarks/Copyright

If the business you are buying has Intellectual property, you may need guidance from a qualified attorney so you and what you are buying is done correctly and therefore you are protected. Intellectual property normally covers the three areas of Patents, Trade Marks and Copyright. Below is a very high level summary of each of the three areas and where you can go for registration and more information.

Patents

A patent is a claim that you, as an inventor, have made something unique and so wish to protect it from use including commercial exploitation by others. A patent doesn't require you to do anything; it simply stops others from using your patent. The means to protect your invention is through applying for a U.S. patent. Because of the complexities, professional assistance from a patent attorney is strongly urged because patent procedures are detailed and technical. A patent search is performed to see if a patent currently exists on the same or nearly the same device and, if not, to make proper application with the Patent Office.

Note: Only attorneys and agents registered with the U.S. Patent Office may represent inventors in related matters. The office has geographical and alphabetical listings of the more than 11,000 registered agents. Only these agents may perform patent searches in the patent office. Inventors or their attorneys can make arrangements with one of those agents. U.S. patents are issued by the Assistant Commissioner of Patents, Washington, D.C.

Additional information is provided in the publication, General Information Concerning Patents and other publications distributed through the U.S. Patent and Trademark Office.

To register a patent, contact:
U.S. Patent & Trademark Office
Mail Stop: USPTO Contact Center
400 Dulany Street
P.O. Box 1450
Alexandria, VA, 22313-1450
(800) 786-9199
Asst. Commissioner for Trademarks, Patent Applications
Washington, D.C. 20231
(800) 786-9199

Also, visit their web site at: http://www/uspto.gov

Trade Marks

Trademarks are names or symbols used in any commerce that is subject to regulation by state government or the U.S. Congress.

State Registration of a Trademark:

Trademarks and service marks may be registered in a state for a term of ten years. For more information about Applications for Registration of Trademark or Service Mark in your state, contact your state government.

Federal Registration of Trademark and Patent

To register a trademark with the US Federal Government, contact:

U.S. Patent & Trademark Office

Mail Stop: USPTO Contact Center
400 Dulany Street
P.O. Box 1450
Alexandria VA 22313-1450
Phone: (800) 786-9199

Also, visit their web site at: http://www/uspto.gov

Caution: Federally registered trademarks may conflict with and supersede state registered business and product names. Businesses are encouraged to check for conflicts with federal trademarks.

Copyrights

Copyrights protect the thoughts and ideas of authors, composers and artists. A copyright prevents illegal copying of written matter, works of art or computer programs. In order to ensure copyright protection, the copyright owner should always include notices on all copies of the work.

Contact:
U.S. Library of Congress
James Madison Memorial Building
Washington, D.C. 20559
(202) 707 9100 Order Line
(202) 707 3000 Information Line

For more information:

http://www.uspto.gov This is the United States Patent and Trade Mark Organization.

http://www.stopfakes.gov/sf_how.asp#category1

http://www.sba.gov/index.html and then use the search feature for "patent" or "trade mark" or "copyright."

Finance Planning Tools

The axiom goes: If you can't measure it you cannot manage it. And so it is with the importance of making financial tracking tools, such as a cash flow forecast or pro forma for the business, and just as importantly, your personal life.

When you first take over the day to day management of the business you have bought, you will be taking on risk as you plan, learn, sharpen your skills, and keep your business functioning, and part of the economy. In Section One we talked about the 7 stages of the business life cycle. However, our immediate goal in this topic is to offer some financial planning tools that may help you grow, maintain, and then build on your business' level of profitability.

If financial planning is not one of your primary skills, there is absolute value in engaging a professional to do this for you. If you engage a professional, the plan should be to make it a long term relationship so you get to know each other, define what help you need, on what basis and frequency, how the data can be collected then moved into a reporting frequency and cycle. Once all this is in place, the data needs to be thoroughly interpreted and analyzed so it gives you a road map of where your business has come from, where it is now, and where it is going.

Below I've touched on three financial tools made of Excel spreadsheets you may find useful for your business. The type of business you build and the industry will determine the final make up of the financial tools you need.

Each of the tools described below is from an Excel spreadsheet or Word document put together by SCORE. You can download these files from my website at http://www.Andrew-Rogerson.com. Once this page loads, on the left hand side there is a menu of options. Towards the bottom choose the option called 'Sample Documents' and you will see different Word and Excel files. Please select the document you need.

---

8 Traits of Serious Buyers

1. They are motivated to buy a business at this time.
2. They know why they want to buy a business.
3. They know specifically what they are looking for and why.
4. They have a specific amount of capital set aside that they are ready to invest.
5. They want to be in business for themselves.
6. They are either unemployed or their current job is not working for them.
7. They are the decision maker.
8. If financing is required, they have the necessary credit score and creditworthiness to get loan approval.

Start-Up Expense Planner

As you look at buying your new business it will be a good idea to know what your initial out of pocket expenses will be so you can make sure you have cash available to cover those costs. The spreadsheet below gives you an example to follow. Obviously change the columns to suit your business.

Item or Service	Quantity	Budget	Actual Cost	Variation	Date bought
Computer(s)	2	$1,000	$700	$300	
Printer - Color Laser	1	$350	$300	$50	
Monitor	2	$350	$400	-$50	
Software (s)	2	$600	$500	$100	
Desks	2	$500	$550	-$50	
Chairs	2	$200	$150	$50	
Fax machine	1	$200	$150	$50	
Phone	2	$200	$150	$50	
Telephone lines	2	$100	$120	-$20	
Filing cabinet - 4 Door	1	$50	$80	-$30	
				$0	
Website Design	1	$600	$600	$0	
Website hosting - 12 months	1	$100	$80	$20	
				$0	
Business cards		$100	$100	$0	
Flyers		$300	$300	$0	
				$0	
Business License		$50	$100	-$50	
Legal fees - to create entity		$500	$1,000	-$500	
Accounting advice		$1,000	$1,200	-$200	
				$0	
Marketing consultant		$500	$400	$100	
Insurance - Business		$400	$350	$50	
Insurance - Auto		$500	$600	-$100	
Total costs		$7,600	$7,830	-$230	

If you would like a template created in Excel to use for your business to track your start up expenses, please go to: http://www.Andrew-Rogerson.com. Once this page loads, on the left hand side there is a menu of options. Towards the bottom choose 'Sample Documents'. After this page displays, look for document # 9. Simply download, complete, save, and monitor it to make sure you are staying within your budget. This tool has been created by SCORE.

Sales Forecast – Year One Planner

The purpose of the Sales forecast tool is to project your expected level of sales once your business opens for customers. The spreadsheet below gives you a sample to follow. A sales forecast is an important financial tool as it forms the basis of other decisions such as budgeting and cash flow forecasts. The more accurately you can forecast your sales, the better informed you will be for the other financial tools you use and create. If you buy an existing business, the seller will have the historical records you can use. If you want to be comfortable doing sales forecasts this may be a useful tool to use and practice.

Fiscal Year Begins	Jan-08												
12-month Sales Forecast													
	Jan-08	Feb-08	Mar-08	Apr-08	May-08	Jun-08	Jul-08	Aug-08	Sep-08	Oct-08	Nov-08	Dec-08	Annual Totals
Cat 1 units sold	50	55	60	80	120	200	400	280	300	330	400	450	2725
Sale price @ unit	100	100	100	100	105	105	110	110	110	110	110	110	
Cat 1 TOTAL	5,000	5,500	6,000	8,000	12,600	21,000	44,000	30,800	33,000	36,300	44,000	49,500	295,700
Cat 2 units sold	100	100	110	130	130	150	180	120	120	120	135	140	1535
Sale price @ unit	100	100	100	100	100	100	100	100	100	100	100	100	
Cat 2 TOTAL	10,000	10,000	11,000	13,000	13,000	15,000	18,000	12,000	12,000	12,000	13,500	14,000	153,500
Cat 3 units sold	40	40	40	40	45	45	60	30	30	35	40	40	485
Sale price @ unit	50	50	50	50	50	50	50	50	50	50	50	50	
Cat 3 TOTAL	2,000	2,000	2,000	2,000	2,250	2,250	3,000	1,500	1,500	1,750	2,000	2,000	24,250
Cat 4 units sold	20	20	20	25	25	25	30	25	25	25	25	25	290
Sale price @ unit	50	50	50	50	50	50	50	50	50	50	50	50	
Cat 4 TOTAL	1,000	1,000	1,000	1,250	1,250	1,250	1,500	1,250	1,250	1,250	1,250	1,250	14,500
Monthly totals: All Categories	18,000	18,500	20,000	24,250	29,100	39,500	66,500	45,550	47,750	51,300	60,750	66,750	487950

If you would like a template created in Excel to use for your Sales Forecasting, please go to: http://www.Andrew-Rogerson.com. Once this page loads, on the left hand side there is a menu of options. Towards the bottom choose 'Sample Documents'. After this page displays look for document #10. Simply download and save the spreadsheet to your computer and use it as necessary. This tool has been created by SCORE.

Profit And Loss Projection

A Profit and Loss Projection is a planning tool to track your projected sales against your costs to run your business and therefore show how profitable you will be. Below is a very basic P&L projection for 6 months using the sales numbers above from the One Year Sales forecast spreadsheet.

	Jan-08	% B/A	Feb-08	%	Mar-08	%	Apr-08	%	May-08	%	Jun-08	%
Revenue (Sales)												
Category 1	5,000	27.8	5,500	29.7	6,000	30.0	8,000	33.0	12,600	43.3	21,000	53.2
Category 2	10,000	55.6	10,000	54.1	11,000	55.0	13,000	53.6	13,000	44.7	15,000	38.0
Category 3	2,000	11.1	2,000	10.8	2,000	10.0	2,000	8.2	2,250	7.7	2,250	5.7
Category 4	1,000	5.6	1,000	5.4	1,000	5.0	1,250	5.2	1,250	4.3	1,250	3.2
Total Revenue (Sales)	18,000	100.0	18,500	100.0	20,000	100.0	24,250	100.0	29,100	100.0	39,500	100.0
Cost of Sales												
Category 1	2,500	50.0	2,750	50.0	3,000	50.0	4,000	50.0	6,300	50.0	10,000	47.6
Category 2	3,000	30.0	3,000	30.0	3,200	29.1	3,600	27.7	3,600	27.7	4,000	26.7
Category 3	1,000	50.0	1,000	50.0	1,000	50.0	1,000	50.0	1,100	48.9	1,100	48.9
Category 4	100	10.0	100	10.0	100	10.0	120	9.6	120	9.6	120	9.6
Total Cost of Sales	6,600	36.7	6,850	37.0	7,300	36.5	8,720	36.0	11,120	38.2	15,220	38.5
Gross Profit	11,400	63.3	11,650	63.0	12,700	63.5	15,530	64.0	17,980	61.8	24,280	61.5
Expenses												
Salary expenses	2,000	11.1	2,000	10.8	2,000	10.0	2,000	8.2	2,000	6.9	2,000	5.1
Payroll expenses	1,500	8.3	1,500	8.1	1,500	7.5	1,500	6.2	1,500	5.2	1,500	3.8
Outside services	300	1.7	300	1.6	300	1.5	300	1.2	300	1.0	300	0.8
Office supplies	100	0.6	100	0.5	100	0.5	100	0.4	100	0.3	100	0.3
Repairs and maintenance	50	0.3	50	0.3	50	0.3	50	0.2	50	0.2	50	0.1
Advertising	120	0.7	120	0.6	120	0.6	120	0.5	120	0.4	120	0.3
Car, delivery and travel	80	0.4	80	0.4	80	0.4	80	0.3	80	0.3	80	0.2
Accounting and legal	500	2.8		0.0		0.0		0.0		0.0	500	1.3
Rent	400	2.2	400	2.2	400	2.0	400	1.6	400	1.4	400	1.0
Telephone	50	0.3	50	0.3	50	0.3	50	0.2	50	0.2	50	0.1
Utilities	45	0.3	45	0.2	45	0.2	45	0.2	45	0.2	45	0.1
Insurance		0.0		0.0	400	2.0		0.0		0.0		0.0
Taxes (real estate, etc.)		0.0		0.0		0.0		0.0	400	1.4		0.0
Interest	250	1.4	250	1.4	250	1.3	250	1.0	250	0.9	250	0.6
Depreciation	300	1.7	300	1.6	300	1.5	300	1.2	300	1.0	300	0.8
Total Expenses	5,695	31.6	5,195	28.1	5,595	28.0	5,195	21.4	5,595	19.2	5,695	14.4
Net Profit	5,705	31.7	6,455	34.9	7,105	35.5	10,335	42.6	12,385	42.6	18,585	47.1

If you would like your own working document so you can do your own projections, please go to: http://www.Andrew-Rogerson.com. On the left hand side there is a menu of options. Towards the bottom choose 'Sample Documents'. After this page displays look for documents #11 & #12. Download the spreadsheet to your computer and use it. SCORE have created this tool.

Other Finance Planning Tools

In addition to the Startup expense spreadsheet, the Sales forecast spreadsheet, and the Personal Budget spreadsheet, a good thing to do before starting your business is to create a Profit and Loss projection for the first year and the first three years. You can also create a cash flow projection so you can understand when you will have to make the actual payments to keep your business open and in good graces with your suppliers, lender, and employees. Good business practices may also include doing a competitive analysis and/or breakeven analysis. If you would like to do these there are spreadsheets available. Finally, if you want to create an initial balance sheet and ongoing balance sheet these documents are also available.

All these documents give you reference points as your business builds, and a financial road map to know you are heading in the right direction or make some adjustments to get to your destination.

Cash flow projection

If you would like a working document, please go to: http://www.Andrew-Rogerson.com. When this page loads, on the left hand side there is a menu of options. Towards the bottom choose the option called 'Sample Documents'. After this page displays look for document #13 & #14.

Breakeven Analysis

If you would like a working document, please go to: http://www.Andrew-Rogerson.com. When this page loads, on the left hand side there is a menu of options. Towards the bottom choose the option called 'Sample Documents'. After this page displays look for document #15.

Competitive Analysis

If you would like a working document, please go to: http://www.Andrew-Rogerson.com. When this page loads, on the left hand side there is a menu of options. Towards the bottom choose the option called 'Sample Documents'. After this page displays look for document #16.

Balance Sheets

If you would like a working document, please go to: http://www.Andrew-Rogerson.com. When this page loads, on the left hand side there is a menu of options. Towards the bottom choose the option called 'Sample Documents'. After this page displays look for document #17 & #18.

Financial Projection Models

If you would like a working document, please go to: http://www.Andrew-Rogerson.com. When this page loads, on the left hand side there is a menu of options. Towards the bottom choose the option called 'Sample Documents'. After this page displays look for document #19 & #20.

If this is all new to you, SCORE provides a great source of information and help. To find a local SCORE chapter go to their website http://www.score.org and search based on your zip code.

Risk Management

In the previous topic we went through budgets and other finance planning tools. Right behind this subject is risk management. Risk management is basically putting a strategy in place that has the primary focus of looking at the operation of a business to try and determine if all the components of the business are operating correctly and in sync with each other. For example, as you start your business you build with growth in sales, happy customers, and employees which flow to the bottom line. When this happens, this is the time when the owner of the business takes his eye off the ball. Overseas trips, golf once a week with his new found business friends, adding the new and latest sports car to the business or running up large bills for no other reason than the business can afford it.

Risk management can mean different things to different people. It's not the goal of this topic in this guide other than to mention it so you are aware it exists and when the time is right in your business to pay attention to it. Create data points, measure the critical performance levels in the business, and manage them; closely.

Risk management can be applied in the early stages of your business to ensure the budgets and limited capital you have to spend are done within tolerance levels. When they move out of tolerance, it's time to address what's happening and bring it in line with what's been planned. For example, it may be agreed that sales and marketing expenditure is $400 per month until gross sales meet a certain level. The risk management aspect would be to monitor that agreement and if sales are not at the correct level but sales and marketing needs $400 per month (or more) then a cut needs to be made in another area.

Another application of risk management is benchmarking industry standards and seeing how your business is performing against those standards. For example, through research you have found that the Cost of Goods for the type of business you operate in your industry is 40% of gross sales. When you look at your business and find your Cost of Goods is 55% of gross sales, you need to do some work to negotiate lower prices as your competitors are doing better than you. And so it goes on.

You may perceive risk management as something a mature business undertakes. But it has different applications for different stages of a business. When you start your business I expect you will not have the time or resources to focus on it. However, if you are getting professional help they should be able to provide this analysis as part of their service at little to no additional cost.

The 5 steps of good risk management are:
1. Risk Identification is deciding the what, how, and when. Data needs to be measured and then made sure all data is collected the same way each time so the results aren't distorted or irrelevant.
2. Risk Analysis involves categorizing risks, deciding the significance of the risk and if it's important enough to spend resources to fix the problem. This is then followed by risk reviews to make sure everyone's on the same page and the problem doesn't reappear.
3. Risk Response Planning is planning what steps to take if an element gets out of alignment.
4. Risk Plan Implementation is establishing an action plan once an event is out of alignment.
5. Risk Tracking and Monitoring involves watching to see if the implementation is working. If the problem persists then it goes back to number one for further risk identification for analysis and resolution.

This topic may sound too advanced for a start up business but understanding its logic and methodology can truly allow you to build a powerful business in a shorter time, and having it ready to sell should a suitable buyer come along.

If this topic is of interest to you and you would like a working document to help you, please go to my website http://www.Andrew-Rogerson.com. On the left hand side of the Home Page there is a menu of options that includes one towards the bottom called Sample Documents. Click on this menu option and once this page displays you will see different Word and Excel files created by SCORE. Documents # 11 & # 12 may help though you are welcome to use any of the other documents.

Finance Options

With all the items on the checklist to take care of, often a key component of the deal is you securing financing.

Most franchisors have a process in place for securing a loan for the buyer. This is the normal process but as a business broker I do have contacts with national, regional, and local lenders who will finance a franchise purchase to a qualified buyer.

To make an application for a loan, you will normally need:

✓ An application form from the lender you will need to complete.
✓ Proof of an acceptable amount for a payment including proof if it is in cash (* See **Note** below.)
✓ A minimum credit score acceptable to the lender (this varies but is about 680 on the FICO and up.)
✓ Supporting documents for the loan such as tax returns, payroll stubs to show previous wages, and income, business plan plus many other documents as it relates to the transaction.

Finance may also be required for funding working capital or Accounts Receivable or assets of the business such as vehicles or office equipment. In some cases, financing can be provided by the franchisor but in most cases it will be provided by a third party.

To minimize frustration, early in the process disclose to the franchisor you will need finance and that it will be a condition on which to make your purchase. The franchisor can then explain their arrangements so you can do the appropriate research to see if the finance is acceptable to you at the right terms and conditions.

Consider securing funding for the downpayment from different sources such as family, friends, banks or credit unions. These are not necessarily typical sources of funds for every buyer, but other options include:
✓ Home equity loan
✓ Local banks
✓ Small Business Administration (SBA)

If you have money in a 401k plan and would like to use this as downpayment to buy a business, more information is available from companies that specialize in this sort of funding. More information is available in Section 8 called "Other finance options."

* **Note**: As we are talking about money, a franchise buyer will need to have a downpayment available, in cash, to buy almost any franchise. If a downpayment is not readily available it is one of the first things I would get in place before talking to franchisors otherwise you may waste a lot of time and energy, and create a lot of frustration not only for yourself but also for others.

If this topic is of interest to you and you would like a working document to help you, please go to my website http://www.Andrew-Rogerson.com. On the left hand side of the Home Page there is a menu of options that includes one towards the bottom called Sample Documents. Click on this menu option and once this page displays you will see different Word and Excel files created by SCORE. Documents #4, #5 & #6 may help though you are welcome to use any of the other documents.

Sources of additional information include:

SBA Loan program:	http://www.sba.gov
Small Business finance:	http://www.vfinance.com
Finance options:	http://www.business.com/Finance.asp
CNN Money:	http://money.cnn.com/index.html
Federal Government Small Business Finance:	http://www.business.gov/guides/finance

"There are risks and costs to action. But they are far less than the long range risks of comfortable inaction."

John F Kennedy

Transaction Documents

The sale of any business involves a large quantity of documents. The more complex the sale, the greater the number of documents to read and process. In simple terms, the documents include those used in the normal course of running the business such as profit and loss statements, property lease, franchise agreement, and business tax returns.

Below is a list of the more common documents broken into three groups.
1. Documents the seller would bring to the transaction
2. Documents the buyer would bring to the transaction
3. Documents needed to be completed during the transaction

This information will allow you to collect the documents you will need and research the ones you are not sure about.

Seller Supplied Documents:

✓ Profit and Loss Statements for the last three years
✓ Balance Sheets for the last three years
✓ Statements of Cash Flow (if available)
✓ Tax returns for the last three years
✓ Sellers Disclosure
✓ List of Fixtures, Furniture & Equipment
✓ Confidentiality Agreement or Non Disclosure Agreement (Discussed in more detail in Section Four.)
✓ Resolutions to Sell
✓ State Sales Tax returns (if applicable)
✓ State Payroll Tax records (if applicable)
✓ List of vendors
✓ Confidential Business Review

Buyer Supplied or Completed Documents:

✓ Signed Confidentiality Agreement
✓ Financial statement to show the buyer has the ability to buy the business or make the down payment they are representing
✓ Resume to show any skill specialties (if the seller or lender requires)
✓ Credit report to assure the seller that the buyer has the ability to get a loan
✓ Buyer's Disclosure Statement

Note: If a business requires a conditional license or permit, for example, a permit that precludes the owner from holding a license if they have a felony conviction, then it would be worth requiring the buyer to make a disclosure so time is not wasted on a transaction that can never close.

Other Documents Used During the Transaction

- ✓ Asset Purchase Agreement or Letter of Intent
- ✓ Counter Offer form
- ✓ Bulk Sale information (if applicable)
- ✓ Inventory final count and value
- ✓ Bill of Sale
- ✓ Landlord Waiver (if applicable)
- ✓ Escrow instructions
- ✓ Asset Purchase Price Allocation (if applicable)
- ✓ Fictitious Name Abandonment form (if applicable)

Sources of additional information include:

www.business.gov
www.findlaw.com
www.lawyers.com
www.copyright.gov
http://www.businesslaw.gov

"People who don't take risks generally make about two big mistakes a year. People who do take risks make about two big mistakes a year."

Peter Drucker

Stock Sale V Asset Sale

I am not an attorney and therefore cannot provide legal advice. My suggestion is that if you need legal advice, please make sure you get it and do all you can to get it from a qualified source. This really applies whether you need legal, accounting, tax or financial planning services. Yes, it does cost money, but the price you pay should save you so much more in either correcting a mistake or spending the time recovering from a self-inflicted problem that now needs professional help to resolve.

Some common legal areas to understand include the following:

Stock Sale vs. Asset Sale

When you buy your business you may have two choices. If the business is a Sole Proprietor, Limited Liability Company (LLC) or Partnership, you can only sell the assets of your business. If your legal entity that holds the assets of the business is a C-Corporation or S-Corporation, then you could have the option of buying the assets of the business or the stock (or shares) of the corporation if the seller is also agreeable. The consensus is that a buyer is much better buying the assets of the business than the stock. If the buyer buys the stock they take ownership of the business "as is." This can be a much simpler and quicker transaction than an Asset sale but it means the buyer takes any liabilities that the business is currently exposed to even if the buyer had no knowledge or involvement in the incident. Liability can be reduced with the seller providing a personal guarantee but I would recommend a buyer obtain legal advice before making any final decisions.

Stock sales are not as common in privately held companies as Asset sales but they are not unheard of as the following table from Pratt's Stats shows.

Total Transactions	Sales Range $	Stock Sales	% of Stock Sales
3658	0 – 1,000,000	422	11.5
937	1,000,001 – 2,000,000	268	28.6
1042	2,000,001 – 5,000,000	499	47.9
799	5,000,001 – 10,000,000	497	62.2
695	10,000,001 – 20,000,000	435	62.8

Make sure an Asset Purchase Agreement or Stock Sale is prepared by a qualified party. There is too much at stake for something not being done correctly.

Advantages of a Stock Sale Vs Asset Sale

Buyer:

1. The buyer doesn't pay sales tax on fixtures and equipment where states have this tax.
2. The current contracts in place with the existing customers, employees and suppliers continue so there is no need to negotiate all over again.
3. No disruption to accounts receivable or accounts payable—just continue business as usual.

4. In about half the transactions, a lower purchase price.
5. Working capital is part of the transaction and already in place.

Seller:

1. No need for the seller to collect the accounts receivable.
2. Seller has sold his legal responsibilities of the corporation.
3. Potential upside on taxes.

Letter of Intent

The use of a Letter of Intent normally happens in more sophisticated transactions. If the deal is straight forward and the seller and buyer seem to be in agreement on the terms of the deal, a Stock Purchase Agreement or Asset Purchase Agreement can be written by a qualified agent. However, if the deal is complex and both parties want to see if there is common agreement on most if not all the terms of a deal, a Letter of Intent allows one party to make a non-binding offer to get feedback from the other party.

Just to be confusing, some parts of the Letter of Intent can be binding. For example, confidentiality clauses or a "no-shop" agreement that indicates the other party will not negotiate with any other party while the Letter of Intent is in play. Letters of Intent are best written and presented by an agent so discussions and counter discussions can take place without the principals in the transaction getting frustrated with each other.

> *"A leader who confines his role to his people's experience dooms himself to stagnation; a leader who outstrips his people's experience runs the risk of not being understood."*
>
> *Henry Kissinger*

Agency

As you look for businesses for sale you will inevitably come across listings being represented for the owner of the business by a business broker or other intermediary. You can also hire the services of a professional to assist you in buying your business. The laws that agents work under are briefly covered below.

- ✓ A **Universal Agent** acts for the Principal for an extended period of time and with broad responsibilities under, for example, a Power of Attorney. A good example is an attorney.
- ✓ **General Agents** are given responsibility for an extended period of time for specific purposes. Examples could include an insurance company or a company managing a person's medical responsibility because they were unable to do it themselves.
- ✓ **Special Agents** are generally hired for a specific transaction or for multiple transactions but for a short period of time. Examples would include a business broker or business intermediary.

10 things to expect from your business broker

If you choose to hire a broker there are many options to consider. To help you make that decision, consider the following.

1. Trust and Ethics.

When buying your business you want to feel assured the Broker/Sales Agent has a strong commitment to trust and ethics so you know your interests are fully protected. Getting an ethical and trust commitment from your Broker/Sales Agent is the most important ingredient. It is critical and should be non negotiable.

2. Real Estate License.

Many states in the US require a Broker/Sales Agent to hold a real estate license in order to represent an owner of property in a sale and be paid for providing that service. In California, a license is issued by the California Department of Real Estate for two types of persons: a Broker and a Sales Agent. A Broker can either work on their own or choose to hire a Sales Agents that work under the Broker.

If you are considering hiring a Broker or Sales Agent, make sure the license they hold is current. For California, this can be checked at the Department of Real Estate website by entering the person's last name and doing a search. The California Department of Real Estate web site is: http://www.dre.cahwnet.gov/index.html. Once the website loads, click on the short cut that looks like

this: After this loads, you can enter the first and/or last name of the Broker/Sales Agent to see if they hold a license.

3. Specialization.

Does the Broker or Sales Agent you are considering hiring specialize in residential sales, business opportunities, commercial real estate transactions or a mix of these? Because of the complexities and differences of each market and their services, most Brokers or Sales Agents tend to specialize in one field.

4. Experience.

Has the Broker/Sales Agent owned and operated a business? Business ownership teaches many skills and requires a unique understanding of what's involved in owning and operating a small business. When detailed negotiations take place between the business owner and a potential buyer, all the options must be explored and fully considered and understood.

5. Accreditations.

Does the Broker/Sales Agent have formal training or education to support the service they provide? There are different types of accreditations with some including the Certified Business Intermediary (CBI) from the International Business Brokers Association, and the Certified Business Broker (CBB) from the California Association of Business Brokers. Make sure the broker you choose has professional training in specialization.

6. Association memberships.

Accreditations are good, keeping up the accreditations is better. To see if a Broker/Sales Agent is a member of their industry association, check the International Business Brokers Association (IBBA) at http://www.ibba.org or the California Association of Business Brokers (CABB) at http://www.cabb.org or find an organization or chapter of a brokers association in your state.

7. Communicates and explains clearly

Buying (or selling) a business requires dealing in financial, legal, industry and other forms of jargon. Are you able to communicate easily and clearly with your Broker/Sales Agent and understand what they are talking about?

8. Network of professionals.

Selling a business often brings together different professionals together such as Accountants, Attorney's, Property Management Companies, Landlords, Escrow officers, Appraisers, Tax Agents, Lenders, Franchisors and Financial Planners. Does your Broker/Sales Agent have professionals he can introduce you to if your business requires that expertise?

9. Testimonials.

What do the past customers have to say about the services of the Broker/Sales Agent?

10. Finance.

Most buyers require some sort of third party finance to buy a business. Is your Broker/Sales Agent able to introduce you to finance professionals who would finance the deal?

Business Valuations

This is an intriguing topic and critical to all buyers who want to buy a business. Interestingly, one of the first questions a buyer wants to know is: *How much does the business cost to buy?* The follow up question is: *How did you arrive at that price?* With the next question: *Is the price negotiable?* As a buyer of a business, you may be interested in knowing a little about valuations so it holds you in good stead when you find a business that is of interest to you.

There is a lot of information available on this topic but here are immediate considerations:
1. Beware of the scams
2. Valuations or appraisals could be required for different parts of the business and they are rarely done by the same appraiser as they each have specialized training. For example, valuations could include the business in its own right, the land and the buildings if owned by the business owner, the machinery and equipment and any intangible items such as trademarks, copyrights and/or patents.
3. The result of the valuation could be different even if the appraisal is done by the same appraiser.

Beware of Scams

There is a cottage industry of sales people calling on business owners and selling a business valuation to business owners. The valuations are overinflated as their purpose is to entice the business owner into paying a fee of $5,000 to $30,000 on the basis the sales person has a buyer interested in the business. They conclude by saying that the owner can't sell their business until they know what it is worth.

Part of the sales pitch and as an inducement to get the fee for the valuation, these sales people offer to take an open listing. This means the owner of the business is free to find their own buyer. However, the sales person offers to advertise and bring qualified buyers (or part of the pitch is that they already have them) and then receive a commission only if the business sells. The business owner thinks this is reasonable for three reasons.

First, the business owner needs a valuation and they are not sure how this done. Second, the sales person only gets paid a commission if the business sells and third, the sales person says he/she has a buyer.

There are two indicators that this is a scam. The first is that the price the business owner pays for the valuation is very high. Second, the sales person suggests their company has a lot of interested buyers and they have a great chance of bringing a qualified buyer to the business owner, when in fact this is highly unlikely.

Some clues that this may not be as good as it seems are that the sales person is either from out of state or they are passing through the area and will not be back for a long period of time. Plus, the sales people tend to use pressure tactics and threats like: "If you are not interested, I will go to your competitor just down the road."

The bottom line is to be aware as these businesses are often listed for sale on the internet so proceed with caution.

Types of Valuations

A lot of business owners don't do a business valuation before listing the business for sale. They have a price they want based on what they may have heard similar businesses sell for, or in some cases, what they will accept if a buyer is willing to pay. In general terms, however, there are three types of valuations:

1. A Brokers Opinion of Value—Costs from $500 to $1,000 depending on the complexity.
2. A Standard Valuation—Costs from $3,000 to $5,000 depending on the structure of the business, the reason and complexity of the valuation.
3. A Full Appraisal—Costs from $7,500 for complex valuations that do or may involve litigation.

To help understand valuations it is necessary to understand Uniform Standards of Professional Appraisal Practice (USPAP). USPAP sets the generally accepted standards for professional appraisal practices in North America, similar in purpose to GAAP which is used by the accounting profession.

A Brokers Opinion of Value is not USPAP compliant. However, if the purpose of the valuation is to establish a listing price for the business and the methods used to determine the Brokers Opinion of Value are reasonable, then it could be argued that this is all the business owner needs. The final price is decided by the market and the ability to locate a buyer willing to pay the price for which the business sells. Additionally, the cost of a Brokers Opinion of Value is not burdensome and may save you the expense of a Standard Valuation or Full Appraisal. A standard valuation and a full appraisal are generally used for valuing businesses that may never be sold but are needed to resolve a legal dispute.

Purpose of the Valuation

To be a little clearer, it is mentioned above that there are three types of valuations: the Brokers Opinion of Value, a Standard Valuation and a Full Appraisal. The type of valuation to choose would depend on the purpose of the valuation. The Brokers Opinion of Value is mainly used by a business owner to understand the listing price of the business.

A Standard Valuation or a Full Appraisal would be requested depending on the reason for the valuation. If a matter is going to court for litigation, generally a Full Appraisal would be requested so there is a thorough examination of all aspects of the business. For example, if a husband and wife jointly own a business and decide to divorce, the husband or the wife may choose to continue to run the business but the other party needs to be bought out. A standard valuation or full appraisal done by a qualified appraiser will examine the financial performance of the business, analyze the economy and industry of the business and make a determination on the value of the business, even though the business will never be sold. The same applies when partners in a business decide to split. A deep analysis of the business is required so the partner leaving the business can be adequately compensated.

The purposes of a Standard Valuation or Full Appraisal therefore could be:
✓ Establishing the value of a minority owner's portion of the business
✓ Agreeing on a value to settle a divorce
✓ Starting or maintaining an employee stock ownership program
✓ Settling a Buy/Sell Agreement
✓ Establish the initial value of the business to start a Buy/Sell Agreement

Valuations are also required by finance companies before they will approve a loan. But the finance companies would order the valuation and define the terms of the valuation. Hence, as I already mentioned, the result of the valuation could be different even if it is done by the same appraiser on the same business because it depends on the purpose of the valuation.

Valuation Methods

Valuations are based on either the Market method, the Cost or Income method or the Asset method—or a combination of any or all of these. Within each method there are different valuation approaches as determined by the appraiser. This may be argued, but for privately held business valuations, the International Business Brokers' Association arrives at the value of a business called the Most Probable Selling Price or MPSP.

The MPSP comes from the Fair Market Value of tangible assets plus intangible assets plus goodwill then plus or minus any other adjustments. Fair Market Value (FMV) is a common standard used by professional appraisers when valuing a business. Business brokers affiliated with the International Business Brokers Association generally use MPSP as the standard. The main difference between MPSP and FMV is that MPSP considers either the buyer or seller or both to be under a compulsion to make a decision, and so this affects the final price they are willing to pay or accept. FMV is the amount that the business would change hands between a willing seller and a willing buyer when neither is under compulsion, and when both parties have reasonable knowledge of the facts of the business.

Discretionary Earnings

When conducting an appraisal for a business, the basis of the valuation generally comes from determining the Discretionary Earnings the business generates, generally over the last three years of the business operating. Discretionary Earnings has different names including Discretionary Cash Flow (DCF) and Owners Discretionary Earnings.

Explaining Discretionary Earnings is a subject in its own right and too much information for this guide. However, if it is an important subject to you and you would like to understand this topic a little more, Section Seven has a topic called "Recasting Financial Statements" and it demonstrates how Discretionary Earnings are calculated. It also includes a template for you to try and calculate Discretionary Earnings along with a sample to show you how it is done.

> *"Risk comes from not knowing what you are doing."*
>
> *Warren Buffett*

Other Types Of Valuations

The most common valuation needed by business owners is someone to value the entire business. However, other valuations are necessary and generally do not include the same person who does your business valuation. These include:

Commercial Real Estate Valuations

When the owner of the business also owns the land and the buildings, a real estate valuation is necessary. It is common to obtain a value for the business and get an approximate valuation or set of comps on the land and building. A formal appraisal to establish a Fair Market Value for the land and buildings is usually needed prior to closing escrow or in order to have a loan approved for the buyer to make the purchase.

Machinery and Equipment Appraisals

If a business is asset-rich (oil drilling equipment, farm machinery, earth moving equipment, trucks, etc.), it may make sense to have a Machinery and Equipment Appraiser put a value on these assets of the business. Sometimes the true value in the business is the assets and this assessment forms the basis of the business operation and its value.

Intellectual Property Valuations

Sometimes the value of a business may be tied up or hidden in a trademark, patent, trade secret or other form of intellectual property such as a Web domain name or recipes. The first step is to make sure it is clear who owns the intellectual property. The second step is to make sure it can be transferred or sold. If this looks good then the next step is to value the intellectual property.

Sources of additional information include:

Valuation data resources:	http://www.valuationresources.com
Intellectual Property education:	http://www.royaltysource.com/education.html
Intellectual Property:	http://www.uspto.gov
Business Valuation Resources:	http://www.bvresources.com
Institute of Business Appraisals:	http://www.go-iba.org/event_links.asp

Professionals You Can Hire

One of your many decisions is what professional help you will need, if any, to start your business. Any help you choose to hire will start with your skill set. If you are a marketing consultant by profession you don't need to hire that skill. If you have family or friends who are attorneys or accountants you've got that one covered.

In the very initial stage of starting your business, my suggestion is to avoid hiring too much professional help. At this stage of your business you are in the fact-finding and exploring phase and your needs may change. To spend money on professional advice to then find it's no longer relevant because you've decided to do something else is not a good return on your investment. Initially gather knowledge, information, and names of good professionals so when the time is right to hire their services, you are clear on the help you need and spend your money wisely.

Attributes

In the next topic we will look at the different type of professionals you can hire. However, here are some thoughts on the type of attributes you may look for in that professional.

Accreditation

If you are looking for a professional with a specific skill set, then their accreditation will tell you the education they have obtained for that specialized skill. There are literally hundreds of three and four letter accreditations. To see if that accreditation is what you are looking for, simply do a Google search. Another option is to find their website and read about their education levels to make sure their academic expertise is what you want.

Compensation

Is the advisor being compensated by commissions on the sale or are they charging you a fee for a service? Some advisors have a combination where they get a fee for a certain part of their time but also can get commission if they make a sale. Fully understand how they are compensated to make sure it makes sense to you.

Business knowledge and experience

Going to college, reading and passing the courses, and networking with small business owners is nice. However, where the rubber hits the road, it is experience that counts. Look for someone who understands the dynamics, pressures, stresses, and responsibilities that business ownership demands. This should be one of the foremost skills you need from any small business advisor. The best way of finding that person probably comes from networking with other small business owners who have "been there and done that."

Expert network

A good advisor should have a strong network of accountants, attorneys, consultants, lenders, and other specialists they can refer to you. Referrals are the main stay of most advisors because the work they do often permeates into other disciplines. Their work is therefore exposed to other professionals that get to know not only the advisor's professional work, but also their reputation.

Goal and style synergy

You may meet many advisors but what you are looking for is *the right one*. If honesty and trust are important to you, that will be the type of advisor that will work best for you. Similarly, as you work with an advisor you will build a relationship, and so it is important the person you are dealing with understands what you are about and is able to communicate clearly. As mentioned earlier, if the advisor just wants to use buzzwords and jargon to inflate their importance, then that may not be the type of advisor you want working with you.

Reputation and references

As a business owner you value word of mouth and your reputation. It is therefore rewarding to thank professionals you think highly of by using their services again or referring them to somebody you know who needs that same service. However, a lot of the work the advisors do is highly confidential so they have to be careful when handing out references. If a referral is given unsolicited from a "happy customer" that you know professionally, that should give you encouragement to further inquire about using that professional's services.

Services you can hire

A lot of business owners are reluctant to hire professionals. Reasons include their belief that the cost is too high, the professional doesn't know as much about their business choices as they do, the business owner cannot readily find the right person, or someone they know used that service and had a bad experience.

If the right professional is hired for the right reason, the value they bring should far outweigh their cost. This value will be in saving you time, not only in terms of hours spent, but giving you back your time so you can spend it on more profitable areas. The two primary reasons though to hire a professional are because of the expertise they bring to solve a problem or providing an impartial perspective to an unexpected situation. The tax, finance, accounting, legal, human resources, and business laws are complex. The right professional can quickly navigate you through these areas.

Here are some thoughts on each of the different types of professionals you may need to hire, how to find them, and most importantly, knowing if they are the right fit for you. I've also included blank templates so you can write down questions that come to mind you may want to ask each of these professionals.

"Dare to risk public criticism."

Mary Kay Ash

Accountant/Tax Advisor

There are three types of accounting professionals a business owner may consider hiring to assist with the sale of the business. These are a Certified Public Accountant (CPA), tax attorney or a personal financial planner. The option chosen will likely come down to cost and the specifics you need to address.

The above list is not to suggest that others can't assist. For example, there are many street-wise and highly skilled bookkeepers who may have intimate knowledge of a business and can readily advise you. However, if you are looking for a professional to hire and you have no existing relationships, then these are the professionals to consider.

Resources for Locating CPAs:

American Institute of Certified Public Accountants	http://www.aicpa.org
Thomas Financial	http://www.thomasonfinancial.com

Tax Attorneys:

Lawyers.com	http://www.lawyers.com
National Association of Enrolled Agents	http://www.naea.org/MemberPortal
Findlaw.com	http://www.findlaw.com

Sources of additional information include:

National Association of Financial and Estate Planners	http://www.nafep.com/index.html
Risk Management Association	http://www.rmahq.org/RMA
Walker Advisory Associates	http://www.waa-online.com/new/waaonline

Accounting/Tax Questions you want to research or ask.

If you have any accounting or tax questions you have been thinking about or they come to mind as you read this guide, write them down here so you can research then at the appropriate time.

Attorney

Just as there are specialists in finance and accounting due to the breadth of the subject, so too are there experts in the different fields of law. It is important that you find an attorney who specializes in the specific area of law you need, in this case, business law. Your attorney will not only be able to guide you through the legalese of starting your business but with any help creating your legal entity such as a corporation, company or partnership.

Resources for Locating Attorneys:

The American Bar Association:	http://www.abanet.org
Your state's Bar Association:	http://www.abanet.org/barserv/stlobar.html
	http://www.lawyers.com

Sources of additional information include:

http://www.abanet.org/public.html
http://www.legalzoom.com
http://www.nolo.com
http://www.lesi.org
http://www.bizfilings.com
http://public.findlaw.com

Legal Questions to Research

If you have any legal questions you have been thinking about or they come to mind as you read this guide, write them down here so you can research them at the appropriate time.

Business Broker or Business Intermediary

Business brokers, also known as Business Intermediaries, provide a range of services to help buyers and sellers enter and exit business ownership respectively. The best reason to use a business broker is that they have an in-depth knowledge of the buying and selling process, and the necessary license which some states require. This advantage can be tremendous as you can engage the services of a business broker to help you find a business for sale, or a franchise, or both. As you work through your business ownership options, it's good to work with the one consultant so they get to know what is and isn't working for you, but most importantly, develop a level of trust so you know your interests are being looked after. If you don't think this is happening, regardless of who you are working with, look for a new broker. Your broker plays a critical role in being a sounding board for you as well as understanding all the processes, forms and relationships you may need.

The International Business Brokers Association (IBBA) is a global organization and has the largest membership of business brokers in the United States. It provides a forum for the industry including education standards for business brokers to obtain accreditation with the designation of Certification of Business Intermediary (CBI).

Sources of additional information include:

International Business Brokers Association	http://www.ibba.org
Murphy Business and Financial	http://www.murphybusiness.com
California Association of Business Brokers	http://www.cabb.org

For the websites of the other State business broker associations go to Page 93.

Business Broker/Consultant questions to research

If you have any questions regarding personal financial planning you have been thinking about or they come to mind as you read this guide, write them down here so you can research them at the appropriate time.

Jargon And Buzzwords

There are different professionals you may engage as you work through your business purchase or indeed once you become a business owner. Each group of professionals tends to have its own business jargon and methodologies. If these terms seem confusing, stop and ask for a clear explanation. Don't let the jargon used exclude you from understanding what's happening – there is no such thing as a stupid question. This is your life and business – make sure it ALL makes complete sense to you. This is your responsibility. As I mentioned earlier, don't forget the glossary of terms at the back of this guide as it may assist you.

Write down industry jargon or buzzwords you want to research and better understand.

End Of Chapter Notes

Use this page to write down notes, ideas and other brainstorming for buying your business.

Assess Your Qualifications

"In order to succeed, your desire for success should be greater than your fear of failure."

Bill Crosby, Comedian and Activist

Introduction

The purpose of this next section is purely to focus on you as the buyer. Up until this part of the guide the focus has been on providing a lot of general information and background so you, as the buyer, will understand a lot of the terms, buzzwords, and processes used in buying and selling a business. However, for you to move forward with confidence through the process, it's important that you now be organized, focused, and know what business opportunity will make sense to you. To do this you are going to look at your personal situation to arrive at the best business options for you to target and research. In order to do this we are going to look at your strengths, weaknesses, interests, and motivation.

As a business broker I receive a constant stream of buyers inquiring about a business who are not qualified to run it, (be it with education, industry knowledge, financial capacity or other criteria), and so they simply burn out from the process and don't achieve their original objective which was to buy a business. Hopefully this section will allow you to arrive at your core strengths, specific interests, financial ability, and risk tolerance to focus your search on finding the right business and enter into business ownership.

This section is about you and your buyer profile. Sections Four, Five and Six cover the process of searching for a business to buy, finding businesses that match your profile and personal preferences, make a deal, close the deal, and move into business ownership. Section Seven then has some suggestions to help you with your first 100 days of business ownership while the last section of the guide, Section Eight has some additional information and tools you may find useful.

It's important that you also understand your profile and interests so you have as much information as possible and can determine the direction you want to go as soon as you can. Business owners, intermediaries, and other professionals will be spending time and resources as you will be as well. The Buyer Profile Questionnaire in conjunction with this guide should enable you to answer a lot of your questions and feel confident (albeit nervous) about the direction you are going. If you're direction isn't making sense, I recommend you step away from the process, as buying a business is not the right place for everyone and is not right for you…at the moment.

Create And Understand Your Buyer Profile

If Section Three is to focus on you by creating a Buyer Profile and then working through a process to arrive at your individual preferences, where do you start?

Buyer Qualification Profile

The start of the process I use is with a form called the Buyer Qualification Profile. A sample of the form is included below.

There is nothing too in-depth about your Buyer Profile other than its primary purpose is to help you narrow down the business ownership options or conversely, eliminate business ownership options that ultimately won't make any sense to you. The benefit of doing this is that it will prevent you from wasting time and money looking at businesses that you really don't have any interest in buying. A couple of examples will make this clearer.

If you have $100,000 cash to invest in a business, if you know that you don't want to work in a retail environment, the business has to be no more than 30 minutes from where you live, and has to have been established at least 5 years with at least 5 employees, knowing this information would help you by excluding businesses that didn't meet that criteria.

Similarly, if you want to buy a business with the above criteria and you find one but you don't have the ability to get a loan to buy the business, if you knew this information before you started do you think this would be helpful?

This is the purpose of the Buyer Profile. To find out what type of business in what type of industry appeals to you as a business buyer, as well as your business, management, personal and financial resources so you have a focus and can pursue relevant opportunities.

Below is the form I use to start the process of peeling back the layers of interest of the Buyer to create a Buyers Profile that works with the Buyers I represent. This information allows both of us to be focused and reduce the amount of time and money wasted trying to find the right opportunity.

Once the buyer completes the form, I then do a consultative session to ask a series of questions and answers. With this information plus the other items covered in this section, we arrive at the Buyers Profile and move forward looking for the right business, with confidence.

Buyer Qualification Profile

CONFIDENTIAL

The more we understand your needs, wants, goals and values, the better we will be able to assist you.

Contact information

Name	
Address	
City, State, Zip	
Home Phone	
Office Phone	
Cell	
Fax	
Email	

Instructions: This is a type on document. First save to your computer, fill in your information and return via email. You can also print and fax it to:

OFFICE:

NAME:
ADDRESS:
PHONE:
CELL:
FAX:
WEB: www.Andrew.Rogerson.com

PERSONAL and BUSINESS INFORMATION

Name _____   Date of Birth _____
Address: _____
City: _____ State _____ Zip _____
U.S. Citizen ☐ Yes   ☐ No
☐ Own   ☐ Rent How long? _____
Telephone Numbers: Home ( )   Work ( )   Cell ( )   Fax: ( )
Email: _____
Best time to call: _____

Education: ☐ High School ☐ Bachelors ☐ Masters ☐ PhD ☐ Other
University or College(s) Attended   _____
Major(s) _____   Year Graduated _____

Employment: Current occupation   _____
Type of Business _____
Title/Position _____
Length of Employment _____Salary_____
Responsibilities: (attach resume if available)

_____

Professional affiliations: _____
Previous employment: _____
Type of Business: _____

Spouse's Current Employment: _____
Type of Business: _____
Title/Position: _____   Length of Employment: _____ Salary: _____

Have you ever owned or operated a business?
☐ Yes   ☐ Full-time ☐ Part-time ☐ No
If yes, explain: _____
What attracts you to owning your own business now?_____
What did you like MOST about your past job or business_____
What did you like LEAST about your past job or business? _____
What do you consider your GREATEST achievement? _____
On the basis of your work experience, your strengths are? _____
Your weaknesses are? _____

Would you enjoy owning a business where you:

Consult ☐ Sell ☐   Market ☐ (check all that apply) your product or service?

How do you rate your sales ability? Weak ☐ Average ☐ Strong ☐ Very strong ☐

Why are you considering a change from employment at this time?

_____

_____

In terms of purchasing a business or franchise I am: ☐ Mildly Interested
☐ Very Interested ☐ Ready to Purchase

Do you have any experience in: ☐ Advertising/Marketing ☐ Public Relations
☐ Sales ☐ Management ☐ Customer Service ☐ Finance

Will you devote full time to your business? ☐ Yes ☐ No

How would you rank your family's support of starting a new business?
☐ Fair ☐ Medium ☐ Good ☐ Very Good
Explain:

_____

_____

Will family members be involved with you in the business? ☐ Yes ☐ No   Whom

_____

_____

How would you rate your following business skills?

Sales	Average ☐	Good ☐	Very Good ☐	Excellent ☐
Management	Average ☐	Good ☐	Very Good ☐	Excellent ☐
Organization	Average ☐	Good ☐	Very Good ☐	Excellent ☐
Financial	Average ☐	Good ☐	Very Good ☐	Excellent ☐
Marketing	Average ☐	Good ☐	Very Good ☐	Excellent ☐
Customer Service	Average ☐	Good ☐	Very Good ☐	Excellent ☐

Rank the most important starting with 1 and the least important 10

Control My Future	____
Build a Business	____
Personal Growth	____
Flexible Time	____
Family Involvement	____
Community Involvement	____
Income Level	____
Build to Sell	____
Be My Own Boss	____
Other	____

Please select the attributes that best describe you.

Amiable	☐	Reliable	☐
Controlling	☐	Competitive	☐
Independent	☐	Hard Working	☐
Outgoing	☐	Results Oriented	☐
Flexible	☐	Money Oriented	☐
Diplomatic	☐	Risk Taker	☐
Persuasive	☐	Open Minded	☐
Leader	☐	Intuitive	☐
Direct	☐	Considerate	☐
Growth Oriented	☐	Understanding	☐
Loyal	☐	Spontaneous	☐

How long have you been researching business and franchise opportunities? _____

How will you know when you have found the right business?
_____

In what geographical area would you like to operate your business?
_____

How soon do you want to start this business? _____

Whatever success you have enjoyed in your past business experience, many people are looking for something different and better; please share the three most significant "changes" that you would like to overcome by owning your own business, being your own boss:
_____

_____

_____

What business categories do you have an interest in? _____

What kind of business hours are you interested in?
Part-time ☐ Full-time ☐ Management ☐

Are you looking for an opportunity with multiple units?
Yes ☐ No ☐

Daily roles you would enjoy:

Managing Employees	Yes ☐	No ☐
Sales prospecting	Yes ☐	No ☐
Marketing	Yes ☐	No ☐
Networking	Yes ☐	No ☐
Customer Service	Yes ☐	No ☐
Providing service quotes & estimates	Yes ☐	No ☐

Please describe below the most important things to you in choosing a business. (These can include, but are not limited to money, success, lifestyle, learning, challenge, fun, personal satisfaction, achievement or anything else that you think is important):

_____

_____

_____

_____

_____

Have you ever been convicted of a felony?   ☐ Yes ☐ No
If yes, explain _____

Have you ever filed bankruptcy?   ☐ Yes ☐ No

Have you ever been an officer in a company that has declared bankruptcy?
                              ☐ Yes ☐ No

Cash Available for investment in a business $

Do you have a source for additional funds without obtaining a business loan?
☐ Yes ☐ No If yes, please explain. _____

Monthly household overhead: $ _____

How will you cover your monthly living expenses as you build the business?

_____

_____

Do you want to supplement or replace your current income? _____

Business Characteristics

My ideal business would look something like this: (check most appropriate answer in each case):

Proven, easily replicated system	☐ important ☐ somewhat ☐ don't care
Recognized business or franchise brand	☐ important ☐ somewhat ☐ don't care
Potential for significant growth	☐ important ☐ somewhat ☐ don't care
Potential for longevity of the business	☐ important ☐ somewhat ☐ don't care
Image of business interested in	☐ professional ☐ don't care
(Check all that apply)	☐ automotive ☐ retail food ☐ service business services ☐ home/personal services
Business location is based at ☐ store	☐ home/office ☐ commercial office ☐ call on customers in their business or ☐ call on customers in their home
Business environment	☐ casual ☐ suit and tie ☐ don't care
Competition would be	☐ high ☐ moderate ☐ low
Customer type desired	☐ repeat ☐ businesses ☐ public ☐ unimportant
Employee type desired	☐ blue collar ☐ white collar ☐ skilled ☐ whatever
Number of employees	☐ 10+ ☐ 5-9 ☐ none to 4
Product versus service	☐ products ☐ services ☐ both
Your cash investment level	☐ $100k ☐ $50-99k ☐ $25-49k
Maturity of business	☐ a mature, well-established business w/strong support and structure ☐ a young, developing business w/good support, more flexibility ☐ a ground floor opportunity, offering the highest potential reward or risk
Who will make decision	☐ me ☐ spouse ☐ other
Management style:	☐ actively involved in all aspects of the business ☐ develop employees & delegate responsibilities
Timeframe for being in business	☐ 3 – 6 mos. ☐ 1- 3 mos. ☐ now
Timeframe for deciding	☐ 3 – 6 mos. ☐ 1- 3 mos. ☐ now
Growth	☐ multiple units ☐ prefer one unit if same monetary success is possible
Your need for personal income	☐ 1+ year ☐ 6 – 9 mos. ☐ 3 – 6 mos.
Hours of business	☐ prepared to work whatever hours needed to launch the business ☐ willing to work nights & weekends ☐ only interested in traditional business hours
Preferred roles in the business	☐ customer service ☐ management of staff ☐ management of operations ☐ prospecting for business, sales of product or service ☐ marketing, networking, developing referral sources

Risk/Opportunity   ☐ want to 'cherry pick' locations or markets by being among the first in my community to open
     ☐ prefer to wait until others are already in business in my market to benefit from their experience

Income   ☐ goal is make the maximum income possible
     ☐ seeking to grow and sell business
     ☐ plan to slow down when goals are met

How do you want your family and friends to perceive your business?
     ☐ Contributes to society
     ☐ My business' tangible assets exhibit my financial success
     ☐ My previous experience was a key factor for entry and success
     ☐ I don't care

FINANCIALS

ASSETS			LIABILITES & NET WORTH		
Cash In Banks (itemize)	$		Notes Due Banks and Others (itemized)	$	
	$			$	
	$			$	
Marketable Stocks & Bonds	$		Taxes Payable	$	
	$			$	
Life Insurance Cash Surrender Value	$		Loans	$	
	$			$	
TOTAL CURRENT ASSETS	$		**TOTAL CURRENT LIABILITIES**	$	
	$			$	
Real Estate Owned	$		Real Estate Mortgages	$	
Other Assets	$		Other Liabilities	$	
	$			$	
Retirement Accounts	$			$	
IRAs	$		*TOTAL NON-CURRENT LIABILITIES*	$	
401k	$		*TOTAL LIABILITES*	$	
TOTAL NON-CURRENT ASSETS	$		**NET WORTH**	$	
TOTAL ASSETS	$		**TOTAL LIABILITES & NET WORTH**	$	

SOURCE OF ANNUAL		ESTIMATE OF	

INCOME		ANNUAL EXPENSES	
Salary		Mortgage Payments	
Bonus & Commissions		Automobile Payments or Lease	
Dividends		Insurance Premiums	
Other Income		Other Expenses	
TOTAL		**TOTAL**	

I certify that the information I have provided on this application is complete and correct. I authorize the release of this information to obtain verification of any of the above information. The purpose of this questionnaire is to compile general information and is not binding upon either part.

THIS IS NOT A CONTRACT

Yes I agree ☐ Name: _____

Phone: ( ) _____

"Most entrepreneurs are merely technicians with an entrepreneurial seizure. Most entrepreneurs fail because you are working in your business rather than on your business."

Michael Gerber

Determine Your Downpayment And Borrowing Ability

Whether or not you want to use the Buyer Qualification Profile, before you start looking for a business to buy, your next step is to understand your financial situation including your capacity to buy a business by getting a loan. There are a number of reasons for doing this and these include:

- ✓ If you find a business that's of interest to you, you will need to know if you make an offer that you have the ability to get a loan to buy the business. As a rule of thumb, you will need to have a downpayment of at least 20% to buy the business plus working capital. Therefore, if a business costs $300,000 you will need a downpayment of $60,000 plus working capital.
- ✓ If you are getting a loan from a bank including an SBA lender, they will require the cash downpayment to be liquid before you apply for the loan, that is, they will not let you show the equity in your house as part of your downpayment then take an equity line of credit against your house from another lender to use as the downpayment..
- ✓ Your next step is to review your credit score. Most lenders are looking for a FICO credit score of at least 680.
- ✓ Lenders are also looking at your ability to operate and manage a business in an industry that matches your skill set. The recent experience in the economy from poor performing business loans has highlighted that money was lent to people with inadequate experience in the industry they chose to operate their business in. Having an up to date resume will help you with that.
- ✓ Once again, if you find a business that's of interest and you want the seller to carry a note, they will want to know how much of your downpayment is cash, how much you can borrow from a lender, your credit worthiness including your credit score. If you have not checked your credit score for some time it would be worth doing before you start your business search so you can tidy up your credit score if there is a problem. To check your credit score you can get a free report once a year from http://www.annualcreditreport.com It is in fact a good idea to run your credit report as you can control who and when this is given to people that are asking. You can also buy your credit report from http://www.freecreditreport.com

NOTE: If you plan on borrowing to buy a business, before you start looking closely at the different business opportunities, I would suggest you talk to lenders to get an idea if you would qualify for a loan, and if so, approximately how much they would lend you. The lender obviously cannot be too definitive as they need to see the business you are buying and how it's performing, but they can give you guidelines which should prove to be very useful.

Determine Your Business Experience

Since August 2008, the SBA has tightened the conditions that lenders are able to offer SBA loans. Part of this tightening has been to require a loan to be approved to a buyer with the necessary industry, business, and management experience to run the business. The SBA found that a lot of loans were given to borrowers that simply did not have the necessary business and/or management experience to run a business they bought in a particular industry.

Once again, if you find a business that's of interest and choose to make an offer, before accepting your offer the seller may request a copy of your resume to get some assurance you'll have the ability based on your work experience to get a loan. If the seller doesn't do this, the lender(s) you are working with will.

As you move through the buying process, I suggest you have a core resume available and then tweak it in case you need to highlight a particular set of management, industry or business skills that relate to the business you wish to buy. I am not suggesting you distort your resume but if you are buying a retail business and have previous retail management experience from an earlier part of your career, make sure this is highlighted in your resume as this is a skill the lender will want to know that you have. A number of buyers I've worked with have had extensive management experience. Their resumes were extensive detailing their experience but did not necessarily highlight the skills they had for a specific business in a specific industry that they were requesting for a loan. Bottom line: Make sure your resume reflects your experience, if it does, as it relates to the business you want to get a loan to buy.

What You Will Need To Buy Your Business

If you are serious about buying a business there are five things you will need to move through the process. You don't need to provide these to everybody who asks, but when you get to a point where it will support your request for more information or show you have the ability to buy the business it's good to have things ready. If there is more than one party who wants to buy that one business, by having these documents ready it will give you an edge.

The documents you need are:

1. Resume

A resume is now an important component for three reasons. First, your resume talks about your industry experience. Second, your resume talks about your business and hopefully management experience. There are many buyers that would like to own a particular business but they simply don't have the requisite skills or ability. Your resume will help address that issue with a seller and their advisor. Finally, most buyers need to borrow to buy a business. A lender will not consider your request for a loan without seeing your resume. Up until recently, credit was freely and readily available but that has now changed. The availability of finance has tightened and so sellers and their agents are reluctant to spend too much time with would-be buyers until they know the buyer can qualify for finance if it is needed.

It's also worth considering having different resumes for different businesses/industries, in case you want to highlight a skill that is important to one business but not important to another.

2. Personal Financial Statement

The need for a Personal Financial Statement mirrors the reason you need a resume. Most sellers and their agents require the buyer to have a minimum net worth and available capital as a downpayment to buy a business. They also require this to be disclosed up front as they don't want to invest the time qualifying, educating, and revealing confidential information to a buyer who is not qualified.

3. Copy of your credit score

Yes – you guessed it. The reason you need a credit score is outlined above. My suggestion is that you pull your credit score and have it available to provide when you feel comfortable providing it. If your credit score is pulled too often in a short period of time, it can lower your score. Plus, if you supply your credit score when you feel comfortable providing it, it puts you in control.

4. Proof of downpayment

This is important to have when it's needed so you can assure a seller and/or a lender you have the downpayment in cash and ready to go. As I have mentioned previously in the guide, lenders are more careful in approving loans and they want to make sure the source of a downpayment is from a readily identifiable source and not coming from a source that is being used to collateralize the loan. For example, if the downpayment is coming from equity in your home, that equity may already be used to approve the loan in the first place – and so it can't be counted twice.

5. Agreement with your significant other or partner

This last one was thrown in for good measure. It's probably the most important but the least obvious. How does your wife, husband, significant other or partner feel about you buying a franchise? The industry you've chosen? Will they work in the business with you? Have you discussed the financial and emotional risks you are taking? The questions are endless. Make sure your partner travels with you on all aspects of this journey. Yes – two heads are better than one, and if you both work through the many variables it will help you both once you get into the actual process of opening and running your franchise. Also, as a business broker when I am consulting with buyers I ALWAYS like the partner to attend any consultations so I can make sure their needs and concerns are addressed and understood. If they aren't on board with you, your chances of success are greatly diminished, plus it adds a great stress on your relationship.

Identify Licensing Requirements

From the work we have done so far in this section, you should have a pretty good idea of the sort of businesses that would be of interest to you, your financial ability so it gives you a price range of businesses to look for, and other personal variables. As you start looking at different businesses for sale, bear in mind that some businesses require a specific license to operate that business. Obviously you need to be an attorney to run a legal practice, a dentist to run a dental practice etc.

A lot of businesses require a license to operate the business. The point of this topic here is to remind you of that so when you inquire about a particular type of business you will want to know if a license is required to operate that business and whether you as an individual need that license or can hire somebody to operate the business for you who has the license. Examples of industries to be aware of include: contractor's license (and this covers a range of skills from a general contractor to electrical contractors to plumbing contractors to landscape contractors etc), real estate agents, child care providers, financial planners/advisors, insurance agents etc. Each business requires a business license to open its doors.

Industry license

Some industries also have a specific license requirement. For example, if you serve or sell liquor you will need the appropriate license. If you sell guns and/or ammunition you will need a specific license. Restaurants in California are also required to have a Health Permit so make sure the business you wish to buy has the license in place and that you know what needs to be done to apply for a license and how long it takes. A lender will not provide a loan if you as the buyer cannot qualify or obtain the necessary license.

Business license

Don't confuse the need to obtain a business license with a specific industry license. A business license is normally issued at the local county level and each business that operates in the county is required to obtain a business license. The purpose is mainly to have a public record for the owner of each business in a county in case legal notices need to be served on the owner of the business. Obtaining a business license is a formality, so don't be concerned about getting this.

Permit

Some businesses in some industries also require a permit to operate the business. It could be a Health Department permit or a permit issued by a Sheriff or local law enforcement agency. For example, where I live in Sacramento, CA the local Sheriff's department issues a dance permit that recognizes that the business will provide dancing to its patrons. Once again, obtaining one of these permits is usually a formality. You just have to know you need it and where you get it from. The seller of the business is the one that can assist you with that.

Five key questions to expect a seller to ask.

1. How much money is available as a down payment?
2. Is the money liquid?
3. How soon do you plan on being in business?
4. Who is the decision maker in the purchase?
5. What is your previous management or business ownership experience?

Understand Lifestyle Changes

If you are planning on going into business ownership, a topic you need to discuss with your significant other and be comfortable with, is how it will impact your lifestyle. If you enjoy keeping your own hours, receiving a consistent income you spend as you wish, interacting with the same people day in and day out, like to play cards or golf with your friends during the week etc then business ownership may not be the best place for you at the moment. Successfully running a business requires discipline. It requires sacrifices, compromises, and a willingness to go the extra yard. It will cramp your style and cause you to have divided loyalties such as whether you spend time with your family and friends or get a project done that will hopefully grow and expand your business....until you get your business established.

A process that may help you with this is to interview some business owners you know. If you want to buy a particular business in a particular industry and know somebody in that business already, that is a great place to start. If you don't have that resource, consider talking with any other business owners you know to get their feedback. What you want to focus on is their experience when they started out – not where they are at now. If they have been running the same business for 20+ years their skills, knowledge, and experience is holding them in great store. When you start your business, this is not the place you will be coming from. Understand the long hours, the living off less money than you're used to, the challenges to your time, and make sure moving into business ownership is right for you.

To help with the above process, a template is available below that captures some questions you could ask a business owner (or two) that you know. My suggestion is not to talk about business questions in general and how they are finding business right now; you want to know what it took when they started so you can learn from their experience. That is the nature of the questions below. To try and understand what they did to grow and establish their business so you understand the lifestyle changes that may be necessary.

Here are some interview questions; make sure you add your own:

How many businesses have you owned and did you start or buy them?

Did your businesses have employees or did you run them on your own?

What were the three biggest challenges you faced when you first owned each business?

As you look back and with what you now know, what would you do differently if you were to move into business ownership today?

Was there an initial period of time you think it took before you felt like your business was under control?

How did you choose the industry and business(es) to own and operate?

How did you finance the start of your businesses?

What advice do you have for me?

Write any additional questions you'd like to ask:

Personal Budget Planner

As you work through your process to buy your business, you may like to review your current personal spending to see if you can make any cutbacks. If you are currently single and have no other responsibilities, it makes sense to see where your current expenditures go and if you can make any cutbacks in the short-term. Conversely, if your family currently has two incomes and will drop to one when you start your business, you may want to do the same by seeing what you can cut back, so you can fund your new business until it becomes profitable. These are questions a lender will indirectly want to know.

To help you do that, review the spreadsheet shown below or if you prefer, create your own in Excel and do some "what-if" scenarios. The choices are all yours, however, I would suggest that starting a new business generally costs more and takes longer than most business owners starting out expect, so discretion is the better part of valor.

	A	B	C
1	Main Item	Current Amount	Revised amount
2	Allowances - kids		
3	Auto - Insurance		
4	Auto - gas		
5	Cash		
6	Charitable contributions		
7	Childcare		
8	Clothes		
9	Education		
10	Entertainment		
11	Gifts		
12	Groceries		
13	Hair care		
14	Household costs		
15	Insurance - House & contents		
16	Insurance - Medical		
17	Medical and dental expenses		
18	Miscellaneous		
19	Pet		
20	Property taxes		
21	Rent/Mortgage		
22	Repairs and maintenance		
23	Taxes		
24	Travel		
25	Utilities - Cable		
26	Utilities - Cell		
27	Utilities - Electricity		
28	Utilities - Gas		
29	Utilities - Internet		
30	Utilities - Phone		
31			
32	Total Per Month		
33	Variation		

There is no specific spreadsheet on my website for this but just copy the layout above into Excel and thereby create your own.

Identify Geographic Location

If the industry or business you are considering does not require a commercial, industrial or retail location to operate from then you can skip this topic. If it does, this is a very important topic to work through as part of your decision making process.

After you have looked at the variables of your finances, business interests, education level, what you want from a business etc one important question left is where you want to own and operate your business. For most buyers the answer is obvious – in the area where they live right now.

Once you start looking at businesses for sale, they will obviously be scattered all over the country (and the world, for that matter). If you have roots in a local community then it makes perfect sense to find a business in that community. Your family and friends will automatically do business with you plus they can be part of your 'team' by encouraging people they know to work with you.

The 'Rule of Thumb' is that most people don't like travelling more than 30 to 45 minutes each way to get to work. Otherwise, the commute in terms of time and cost of gas becomes too high. Keep this in mind as you work through your variables. If you find a business you really like that is more than 45 minutes from where you currently live, make sure you want to spend the time knowing more about the business as when it comes to decision time, you probably won't move forward with the transaction as one of your main reasons will be is that it is too far from where you live; especially if the business requires you to travel to it every day.

Assemble Your Team

This is the end of Section Three and so we move into Section Four which starts the process of searching for available businesses for you. Before we move into that Section, this would be the place for you to finalize any members you wish to have on your team so you know who they are, checked they are ready and willing to help, and each party has clear expectations on how they help.

To finalize the members of your team, you may like to go back and revisit the topic in Section Two called 'Professionals you can hire.' The purpose of that topic was to highlight the different professional skills available so you could decide if you wanted any of those skills to be available to help you.

Make your final selection on the basis that this will be a long term relationship. If a professional is not working for you there is no problem making a change; in fact it makes no sense other than to do that. The downside is that finding a replacement can take time and it may not be when you have downtime to do this but need that service now, or it means you may lose momentum or the opportunity you have been waiting for.

To find the professionals you need the best place to start looking is with your immediate family and friends, and people you trust. Your family and friends know you and what you're about and should be able to help and from their circle of influence suggest some people for you. If this doesn't address your need, there are some suggested places to go back in Section Two.

In deciding who these people should be, take into consideration:
1. The skills they bring; you don't want someone with the same skill set if it clashes with your own.
2. A skill set that compliments and complements your own skills and that you believe you are lacking. To be clear, it's important that when you hire somebody to work with you that your working relationship is relaxed. We all have our own personality, style, habits and ways of doing things. Because this is your business, make sure the person you hire understands how you work. It's their responsibility to adjust; not yours.
3. The amount of time they have to help you and whether they will be readily available.
4. The costs involved in hiring the experts you need.
5. Whether you like it or not, one of the most important skills you will want from these people is emotional support and empathy in that they understand what you are going through and their advice is in your best interest and your best interest only. But most important of all, you want someone that will give you an honest answer to tough questions.

Use the following chart to write down the names of primary and secondary people you need for your team.

Service required	Option 1	Option 2	Option 3
CPA/Accountant/Book-keeper			
Attorney			
Business Broker or Intermediary			
Marketing Consultant			
Mentor			
Personal Financial Planner			

End Of Chapter Notes

Use this page to write down notes, ideas and other brainstorming for buying your business.

Section Four

Search for the Best Business

"If we knew what we were doing it wouldn't be research."

Dr. Albert Einstein

Introduction

This section now moves into the process of seeing what businesses are for sale, deciding if they match your Buyer Profile, and your next steps.

At this point in your journey you should be feeling good about yourself. With the work you've done and the foundations you've built, everything should be making sense to you. This includes the industry, business, and management skills you have, your financial ability to buy a business you can afford, and service any loan payments on the business. At the same time, keeping all of this within in the comfort of your ability to meet your personal responsibilities while you settle into business ownership. This could include responsibilities such as mortgage payments. If you have concerns or outstanding questions I would suggest you research and understand those now. Once you move into the search process, it will take a lot of time and follow up plus you will incur costs be it just the gas and wear and tear on your car. However, if you find a business of interest and you hire professional help to assist, there will be a financial cost to this part.

Search For The Best Business

There are many places to search for a business that is for sale. Before we move into researching those variables, here are a couple of additional thoughts to consider.

You may choose to share your interest in business ownership with family and friends. By doing this you may all of a sudden find out certain businesses are for sale. If you know the owner of the business you may be encouraged to go and talk to them or, if you don't know the owner, others may offer to talk to the seller for you. Be careful accepting help from people who are not very familiar with your situation. Once people find out you are interested in business ownership you may find all sorts of businesses offered to you. My suggestion is to keep your Buyer Profile handy and try to stay within those parameters. Do not be closed to new ideas but it's important to buy the right business for the right reason rather than buy a business for sale simply because a family member or friend recommends it.

In a similar vein to the above, if you have a clear indication from the Buyer Profile of the type of business you would like and you know "the perfect business" but it's not for sale, should you approach the owner to see if he wants to sell?

The answer to the above question is – absolutely. However, I would suggest it involves a strategy and the strategy is that you do not approach the seller directly, you have a third person such as a business broker or intermediary do this for you. There are many reasons for making this suggestion. If you have an intermediary do this for you they include:

- ✓ An intermediary can be a firewall or break point between the owner and the buyer. If the buyer goes direct to the owner and says something or comes across in a manner that frustrates or upsets the owner, any potential transaction is unlikely to happen.
- ✓ An intermediary can introduce themselves and see the response from the owner. A lot of owners simply have not seriously thought about selling their business. If an intermediary comes from out of nowhere to see if they are interested, their reaction can be a wide gamut from annoyance to relief, to suspicion to confusion about the next steps etc. The first thing the owner of the business will want to do is work out the authenticity of the intermediary. If they feel the intermediary is genuine, their next step will be to ask for time to think about the idea. Once they have done that they will possibly not be sure of their next step – so it will fall to the intermediary to call back and re-establish where the owner is at and if he has any genuine interest to sell. If he does have an

interest to sell, initially it will be on the terms and conditions of the owner, which may prove too high for you as the buyer. However, if the owner is interested, there is a delicate process to move through the transaction and having an intermediary guide you through it is the best way to go.

✓ Having a business owner and buyer work direct with each other is difficult at the best of times. Each party generally does not have a lot of experience negotiating and handling a transaction including the necessary legal documents, what disclosures to use at different stages in the transaction, what process to use to open escrow, negotiating with the third parties such as a lender, landlord, franchisor and other interested parties.

If you've decided to start your search for a business that is for sale there are a number of places to try. In years gone by the usual method was to look in the local newspaper in the Financial section of the Business Opportunities or businesses for sale. This method has pretty much dried up due to the arrival of the Internet. What has replaced the Financial section of the local newspaper is a website called Craigslist. Most of the listings on Craigslist are very simple businesses. Be careful if you follow up with a seller as some of the information is not accurate as the owners of the business do not present the financial information that would be acceptable to a lender or other interested third party that is exposed to some risk in the transaction.

If you choose to search the web for listings be aware there are many different websites available. The primary service the website is providing is letting you know a business is for sale. They do not check any of the financial material or other claims of the owner or seller so extreme caution is necessary. Some business owners prefer to sell the business themselves rather than use an intermediary. Like people selling their own house, these are called FSBO's or For Sale By Owner. As I mentioned above, dealing directly with a FSBO warrants caution as the FSBO probably hasn't sold too many businesses before and won't be familiar with the process and therefore how to complete the transaction. A local escrow company I use in Sacramento suggests that for every one deal that closes when a business broker handles the sale, six deals collapse when an owner and buyer try to close a transaction themselves.

There are a large number of websites that carry listings with businesses for sale. Some are commercial websites that charge the owner or listing agent of the business a fee to post their listing while some are websites that belong to an association that professional intermediaries join. For example, the International Business Brokers Association (IBBA) has a membership of approximately 1800 business brokers from around the world. The vast majority of members live in the US and Canada but there are members from Australia, New Zealand, Hong Kong, Greece, and England to name a few.

In California, there is also a State association called the California Association of Business Brokers (CABB.) This association is similar to IBBA but at a state level. There are other state associations and these are listed on the next page. The main benefits of dealing with a business broker from IBBA or a state association is that they have a Code of Ethics they must follow as members, a level of professional training that enables them to successfully handle the successful change of possession from a seller to a buyer, plus many additional professional resources such as access to lenders, escrow companies, accounting, legal, and tax planning resources.

Listed below are some websites you can use to see what businesses are currently for sale. Some websites are subscription-based as the owners or the business broker of some businesses want to more closely manage their listing and so won't disclose any details until the buyer shows they have the education, management skills, and financial resources to buy the business.

Websites with businesses for sale:

Andrew Rogerson's website	http://www.Andrew-Rogerson.com
Restaurant eXchange	http://www.restx.com
Murphy Business and Financial	http://www.murphybusiness.com
Bizbuysell	http://www.Bizbuysell.com
Restaurants	http://www.RestMart.com
Merger Network	http://www.Mergernetwork.com
Bizquest	http://www.Bizquest.com
USA Biz Mart	http://www.USABizMart.com
BizBen (California businesses only)	http://www.Bizben.com
Inc. Magazine	http://www.inc.com
Businesses for sale	http://www.BusinessesForSale.com

Other websites with businesses for sale:

International Business Brokers Association	http://www.ibba.org

There are also a lot of US states with Business Broker Associations. The ones with Businesses for sale include the following:

Arizona Association of Business Brokers, Inc.	http://www.azbba.net
California Association of Business Brokers, Inc	http://www.cabb.org
Colorado Association of Business Intermediaries	http://www.cabisource.org
Georgia Association of Business Brokers, Inc	http://www.gabb.org
Midwest Business Brokers Association	http://www.mbbi.org
Michigan Business Brokers Association	http://www.mbba.org
New York Association of Business Brokers	http://www.nyabb.org
Ohio Business Brokers Association	http://www.obba.org
Pennsylvania Business Brokers Association	http://www.pennbba.com
Texas Association of Business Brokers	http://www.tabb.org

Do I Have The Qualifications And Finances To Enter This Industry?

Once your search uncovers a business (or businesses) of interest, the buyer normally wants as much information about the business as possible. My suggestion, before you do that, is to do a little background research. You will probably need more information about the business in order to complete this step, but it's important that you understand all of the following.

Does the business require any specific education?

Some industries require a specific education in order to operate them. Obviously to be an attorney you need to pass the State Bar exam. To be a Certified Practicing Accountant you need to not only pass an exam but also meet experience and education requirements established by the relevant Board of Accountancy Board that has jurisdiction over the area you live. To operate a Physical Therapy business you need to meet certain education standards. To run a preschool in California the Department of Social Services requires certain education levels. To operate a California Closet franchise you need to have an MBA. And so it goes on. The bottom line is that you want to know if a particular business has education requirements you can meet to you know if you will qualify to own and operate the business.

Does the business require any specific license to operate?

A lot of industries have Federal, State or County license requirements or in some cases, a combination of all of them. These are not the standard business licenses but specific education and/or experience requirements.

For example, the construction business requires a license to operate in the business. In California, this license is controlled by the State Contractors License Board. If you had an interest in buying a business that requires a contractor's license you would want to understand the process and how quickly you could get your license or risk having the business you bought being closed down.

Another example is the finance industry. The Securities and Exchange Commission (SEC) require training and passing exams to receive a security license. There are different licenses required for giving professional advice on a range of investment products.

Another example is the child care industry. In California there are education requirements for certain licenses. If you had an interest in buying a preschool you would want to know you would qualify to get that license or risk having the business you bought being closed down.

Other examples of businesses that require a license include a liquor license if you want to serve alcohol in a restaurant, firearms if you want to sell guns and/or ammunition, a gambling permit, for example, if you want to run a bar with slot machines, etc.

If you have a conviction on your record, it may preclude you from getting that license in the first place. Additionally, it may preclude you from getting a loan, especially through the SBA, if you declared a bankruptcy previously.

Check these things out as it can save wasting a lot of time and frustration not only for you but also for others. The seller of the business or the broker will be able to help with this information on your first inquiry with them.

Do you have the down payment and credit score?

Once you get through the education and license requirements, the next thing to check is that you have the necessary cash, or if you plan to borrow, down payment to use to get a loan to buy the business. As a business broker I see so many buyers inquiring about a business yet they have no financial capacity to do a deal. One of the problems I see is that buyers don't want to disclose their personal financial situation because it is sensitive information. This is more than reasonable, but the argument goes in reverse in that it's not reasonable to expect the owner of a business to disclose confidential information about his business being for sale to someone that doesn't have the financial capacity to either pay cash for the business or qualify for a loan in order to buy it.

This is the reason business brokers require a personal financial statement as part of the Confidentiality Agreement as they want to be sure the buyer is qualified.

An extra step I take when working with a buyer is to have them talk to banks and financial institutions that do SBA loans. My goal is to have the buyer pre-approved for an SBA loan so when they find a business they are qualified to buy; they are further into the process. This helps three ways. First, it generally means the seller of a business will accept an offer from a buyer that is pre-approved ahead of a buyer who is not. Second, it demonstrates to the seller that the buyer is preapproved and so has a greater chance of closing the deal, and third, it shows the seller and his business broker that the buyer is serious as they have spent time working with an SBA lender.

As a buyer, making sure you have the qualifications and finance in place before you start your search can greatly reduce missteps, wasting time, and creating frustration not only for the sellers and business brokers you work with, but more importantly, yourself.

Review Blind Business Summary

If you are working with a professional business broker or intermediary, they will invariably produce a high level summary of the business. It has different names including Blind Executive Summary, Blind Confidential Business Review or Blind Confidential Memo.

In essence it's designed to provide the basic but important components of the business so you as the buyer can decide if you would like more information. This document also serves as a means to introduce you to either the owner of the business or the business broker representing the business owner. One of the pressure points between the buyer and the owner is that the buyer wants as much information as possible about the business so they can decide if it's of interest to them. Conversely, the seller doesn't want sensitive information provided to just anyone as it could be a competitor using the opportunity to gain inside information. Equally, the seller of the business doesn't want the employees, landlord, suppliers, lender or other sensitive party finding out the business is for sale in case it damages the business.

Below is a sample of a Blind Executive Summary that I use for my business listings. When you get this document, your goal is to go over it and see if the business matches the criteria you've established in your Buyer Qualification Profile.

If this information does, the broker or seller representing the business will want you to complete, sign, and return a Non Disclosure Agreement which we'll explain in more detail in the next topic.

Rogerson Business Services

Broker: Andrew Rogerson CA DRE# 0175716(

Reference: _____ (916) 570-2674

P&L ☐ Fed Tax ☐ Sales Tx ☐ F&E ☐ Lease ☐

PRICE AND TERMS

Business Price: _____
Inventory: _____
Real Estate: _____
TOTAL LISTING: _____ -
Buyer Cash Required: _____
Debt Service, approx: _____

ESTIMATED VALUES

Fixtures & Equipment: _____
Leasehold Improvemts: _____
Real Estate: _____
Est. Inventory at Cost: _____

OPERATIONS INFO

Ownership form: _____
Years established: _____
By present owner: _____
Reason For Selling: _____
Number days open: _____
Business hours open: _____
License required: _____

LEASE INFO

Total Rent: _____
Deposits: _____
Square Feet: _____
Lease Expires: _____
Options to Renew: _____
Parking: _____

EMPLOYEE INFO

Number of owners work: _____
Hours worked weekly: _____
Number of managers: _____
Manager's Salary: _____
Total payroll/wages: _____
Employees full time _____ Part: _____

Unprotect

Protect

Andrew Rogerson
Service with Ethics
Murphy Business & Financial
Sacramento Area Business Expert
www.Andrew-Rogerson.com

Caution: You could be held liable for disclosing confidential information to unauthorized parties which results in damages to the owner or their brokers

Confidential   Confidential

Confidential   Confidential

REMARKS

SUMMARY OF INCOME

Period				
Gross Income				
Cost of Goods				
Gross Profit	-	-	-	-
Profit Margin	%	%	%	%
Other Income				
Expenses				
Net Before Tax	-	-	-	-
ADD BACK:				
ADJUSTED NET:	-	-	-	-

Complete And Return The NDA

If you are working with a qualified business broker, they will not provide additional confidential business information to you until you have completed, signed, and returned a Non Disclosure Agreement (NDA) or sometimes called a Confidentiality Agreement.

The reason for this is simple and straightforward. The owner of the business does not want customers, employees, competitors or suppliers to find the business is for sale. With a lot of businesses, if this was to happen the business would close down very quickly so confidentiality is a very sensitive matter. By signing and returning the NDA you are agreeing not to discuss any details of the business with anyone other than your professional advisors. This confidentiality would include them not discussing it with anyone. If you breach the confidentiality and it damages the business, you run the risk of the owner of the business suing in a court of law to recover the extent of the damage your disclosure caused.

In addition to signing and completing the NDA, some brokers and/or the owner of the business will not disclose any information until you also complete a financial disclosure to show you have the ability to buy the business. Some buyers are not comfortable with this process but it's important you put your feet in the shoes of the seller. If they disclose a lot of confidential information to a party that cannot buy the business they are simply taking a risk that doesn't make sense to take.

Confidentiality is an extremely important responsibility when buying a business. If you have questions about this issue you are welcome to email me at info@andrew-rogerson.com

Below is a sample NDA that is used in my office. As you can see, the document is detailed and asks for lots of information. All this is to protect the owner of the business and their asset they have built over many years of hard work, and to make sure that you, as a buyer are qualified to buy the business.

ACKNOWLEDGEMENT OF INTRODUCTION AND CONFIDENTIALITY AGREEMENT

The undersigned, individually and on behalf of any affiliated prospective buyer, acknowledges being introduced to the business identified herein by xxxxx **Services, Broker.** The undersigned request information on the following business:

_____ ("Business"). Such information shall be provided to the undersigned for the sole purpose of entering into discussions with Seller of said Business for the possible purchase by the undersigned of all or part of the stock or assets of the Business. As used herein, the term Buyer ("Buyer") applies to the undersigned and any partnership, corporation, individual, or other entity which the undersigned is affiliated. The undersigned agrees as follows:

1. **NON-DISCLOSURE OF INFORMATION:** The undersigned acknowledges that Seller desires to maintain the confidentiality of the information disclosed. ***The undersigned agrees not to disclose or permit access to any Confidential Information without the prior written consent of Seller, to anyone other than Buyer's, legal counsel, accountants, lenders or advisors to whom disclosure or access is necessary for Buyer to evaluate the Business, provided that they are not one of Seller's employees, customers, landlords, suppliers, or competitors.*** Disclosure of Confidential Information shall be made to these parties only in connection with the potential acquisition of the Business, and then only if these parties understand and agree to maintain the confidentiality of such Confidential Information. The undersigned shall be responsible for any breach of this Agreement by these parties, and neither Buyer nor these parties shall use or permit the use of Confidential Information in any manner whatsoever, except as may be required for Buyer to evaluate the Business or as may be required by legal process. If the Buyer does not purchase the Business, Buyer, at the close of negotiations, will destroy or return to Broker (at Broker's option) all information provided to Buyer and will not retain any copy, reproduction, or record thereof.

2. **DEFINITION OF "CONFIDENTIAL INFORMATION":** The term "Confidential Information" shall mean all information, including the fact that the Business is for sale, all financial, production, marketing and pricing information, business methods, business manuals, manufacturing procedures, correspondence, processes, data, contracts, customer lists, employee lists and any other information whether written, oral or otherwise made known to Buyer: (a) from any inspection, examination, or other review of the books, records, assets, liabilities, processes, or production methods of Seller; (b) from communications with Seller or its directors, officers, employees, agents, suppliers, customers or representatives; (c) during visits to Seller's premises; or, (d) through disclosure or discovery in any other manner. However, Confidential Information does not include any information which is readily available and known to the public.

3. **DISCLAIMER OF BROKER'S LIABILITY AND BUYER'S RESPONSIBILITY:** When business brokers take a business to market, they receive information about the business from the Seller, usually including, but not limited to, tax returns, financial statements, equipment lists and facilities leases. Based on information provided by the Seller, brokers often prepare a summary description of the business which may include cash flow projections, an adjusted income statement, or a seller discretionary cash flow statement. Buyer understands that the Broker does not audit or verify any information given to Broker or make any warranty or representation as to its accuracy or completeness, nor in any way guarantee future business performance. Buyer is solely responsible to examine and investigate the business, its assets, liabilities, financial statements, tax returns, and any other facts which might influence Buyer's decision to purchase or the price Buyer is willing to pay. Any decision by Buyer to purchase the Business shall be based solely on Buyer's own investigation and that of Buyer's legal, tax and other advisors. Broker urges Buyer to obtain independent legal and tax counsel.

4. NON-CIRCUMVENTION AGREEMENT: The Seller has entered into an agreement providing that Seller shall pay a fee to listing broker if during the term of that agreement or up to twenty-four months thereafter, the Business is transferred to a buyer introduced by listing broker or a cooperating broker. ***Buyer shall conduct all inquiries into and discussions about the Business solely through Broker and shall not directly contact the Seller or the Seller's representatives.*** Should Buyer purchase all or part of the stock or assets of the Business, acquire any interest in, or become affiliated in any capacity with the Business without Broker's participation, or in any way interfere with Brokers' right to a fee, Buyer shall be liable to listing broker or cooperating broker for such a fee and any other damages including reasonable attorney's fees and cost.

5. FURTHER TERMS: ***Neither Buyer nor Buyer's agents will contact Seller's employees, customers, landlords, competitors or suppliers without Seller's consent.*** For three years, Buyer shall not directly or indirectly solicit for employment any employees of Seller. Broker may act as a dual agent representing both Buyer and Seller. Seller is specifically intended to be a beneficiary of the duties and obligations of this Agreement and may prosecute any action at law or in equity necessary to enforce its terms and conditions as though a party hereto. Seller may assign this Agreement to any new ownership of the Business. This Agreement can only be modified in writing, signed by both Broker and Buyer. Waiver of any breach of this Agreement shall not be a waiver of any subsequent breach. This Agreement supersedes all prior understandings or agreements between the parties with respect to its subject matter. This agreement shall be construed under and governed by the laws of the State of California. If Buyer is a corporation, partnership, or other such entity, the undersigned executes this Agreement on behalf of Buyer and warrants that he/she is duly authorized to do so. **Buyer acknowledges receipt of a fully completed copy of this Agreement.**

Buyer Signature	**Date**

Company

Street Address

City, State, ZIP

California Association of Business Brokers
Professional Service since 1987
Agency Disclosure and Agreement

BUSINESS_____ **BROKER**_____

Agency and Dual Agency: On the reverse of this form is printed a portion of California Civil Code section 2079.16, which requires disclosure of some concepts and definitions concerning the relationship between a principal and an agent in the sale of certain residential real estate. While the listing and sale of a business is not a transaction requiring the use of the form prescribed by that Code section, the information provided is completely applicable to the business sale context as well, and you are requested to read it carefully and acknowledge that you have been advised of its contents.

When a broker lists a business for sale, the broker becomes an "agent" representing the seller. The same broker also often works with prospective buyers, and by the nature of that relationship, becomes a buyer's agent as well; this is called "dual "agency." Although a buyer and seller are sometimes represented by different agents of the same brokerage firm, this is also a dual agency, because the broker who employs each of the agents is really the agent for both parties.

Full Disclosure: Under California law, the buyer and the seller of a business are each required to fully and fairly disclose to the other, any and all information which is known to that party, or reasonably should be known, and which may or will be "material" to the other party's decision to enter into the transaction. An agent must fully disclose all relevant information known to the agent to the party or parties that the agent represents. An agent, whether acting only for one party, or as a dual agent, must make the same such disclosures to the other party, or to the other party's agent and cannot withhold any material information which such agent may know, or in the exercise of reasonable diligence, should discover.

Price and Valuation: There is an exception to the rule that a dual agent must disclose all information in his or her possession. In representing both seller and buyer, the agent shall not, without the express permission of the respective party, disclose to the other party that the seller will accept a price less than the asking price or that the buyer will pay a price greater than the price offered, even though there otherwise might be a duty to do so. Likewise, a broker acting as a dual agent will not disclose valuations or appraisals prepared by the broker for the seller (but must disclose any comparable sales figures which may have been a major factor in such evaluation), nor the contents of any previous negotiations, contracts or offers between either the buyer or seller and any other parties. This is the only way negotiations can be conducted when the broker represents both the buyer and the seller.

Acknowledgment of Disclosure and Agreement to Dual Agency: Each party by signing below, acknowledges and agrees that:

1. The party has carefully read and fully understands the matters discussed above, as well as the language of the statute quoted on the reverse of this form, and has had the opportunity to ask questions and/or to seek the advice of legal counsel prior to signing below.

2. The seller consents and agrees that the Broker representing said party may, in his discretion, act as an agent for any buyer or prospective buyer as well as for the Seller, as explained above and on the reverse hereof, and agrees to the conditions stated above.

3. The Buyer consents and agrees that the Broker representing the Seller will continue to do so even though said Broker will also represent the Buyer as a dual agent, understands all of the information stated above and on the reverse hereof and consents to such dual agency.

    THIS FORM MAY BE SIGNED IN COUNTERPARTS. NOT ALL SIGNATURES ARE REQUIRED TO APPEAR ON THE SAME COPY. FACSIMILE SIGNATURES ARE ACCEPTABLE AND BINDING.

SELLER(S):   BUYER(S):

_____ _____   _____ _____
Signature   Date   Signature   Date

_____   _____
Name (print)   Name (print)

_____ _____   _____ _____
Signature   Date   Signature   Date

_____   _____
Name (print)   Name (print)

_____ _____   _____ _____
Agent for Seller   Date   Agent for Buyer   Date

   **Excerpt from CALIFORNIA CIVIL CODE § 2079.16**

SELLER'S AGENT: When you enter into a discussion with a real estate agent regarding a real estate transaction, you should from the outset understand what type of agency relationship or representation you wish to have with the agent in the transaction.

A Seller's agent under a listing agreement with the Seller acts as the agent for the Seller only. A Seller's agent or a subagent of that agent has the following affirmative obligations:

To the Seller: A fiduciary duty of utmost care, integrity, honesty, and loyalty in dealings with the Seller.

To the Buyer and the Seller:

  (a) Diligent exercise of reasonable skill and care in performance of the agent's duties.
  (b) A duty of honest and fair dealing and good faith.
  (c) A duty to disclose all facts known to the agent materially affecting the value or desirability of the property that are not known to, or within the diligent attention and observation of, the parties.

BUYER'S AGENT: An agent is not obligated to reveal to either party any confidential information obtained from the other party that does not involve the affirmative duties set forth above.

A selling agent can, with a Buyer's consent, agree to act as agent for the Buyer only. In these situations, the agent is not the Seller's agent, even if by agreement the agent may receive compensation for services rendered, either in full or in part from the Seller. An agent acting only for a Buyer has the following affirmative obligations.

To the Buyer: A fiduciary duty of utmost care, integrity, honesty, and loyalty in dealings with the Buyer.

To the Buyer and the Seller:

  (a) Diligent exercise of reasonable skill and care in performance of the agent's duties.

(b) A duty of honest and fair dealing and good faith.

(c) A duty to disclose all facts known to the agent materially affecting the value or desirability of the property that are not known to, or within the diligent attention and observation of, the parties. An agent is not obligated to reveal to either party any confidential information obtained from the other party that does not involve the affirmative duties set forth above.

AGENT REPRESENTING BOTH SELLER AND BUYER: A real estate agent, either acting directly or through one or more associate licensees, can legally be the agent of both the Seller and the Buyer in a transaction, but only with the knowledge and consent of both the Seller and the Buyer. In a dual agency situation, the agent has the following affirmative obligations to both the Seller and the Buyer:

(a) A fiduciary duty of utmost care, integrity, honesty and loyalty in the dealings with either Seller or the Buyer.

(b) Other duties to the Seller and the Buyer as stated above in their respective sections.

In representing both Seller and Buyer, the agent may not, without the express permission of the respective party, disclose to the other party that the Seller will accept a price less than the listing price or that the Buyer will pay a price greater than the price offered.

The above duties of the agent in a real estate transaction do not relieve a Seller or Buyer from the responsibility to protect his or her own interests. You should carefully read all agreements to assure that they adequately express your understanding of the transaction. A real estate agent is a person qualified to advice about real estate. If legal or tax advice is desired, consult a competent professional.

Business Name _____   _____ _____ _____ _____
                                                             initials initials initials initials

BUYER PROFILE FOR: _____   Email: _____
                          Please Print Name

Home Address: _____ City: _____ State: _____ Zip: _____

Home Phone: _____   Work Phone: _____

Fax: _____   Cell Phone: _____

How did you hear about us? _____ If Internet, which website?_____

We provide each seller the following confidential facts about you prior to releasing any information about their business.

BACKGROUND INFORMATION:

Are you currently employed? _____ If so, in what industry and what position _____

Please give a brief description of your responsibilities: (Plan to prepare and submit a formal Resume for consideration.)
_____

Please list the industries in which you've worked and the positions you've held:
_____

Does your spouse work? _____ Full time? _____ Industry and position? _____

Do you own or have you ever owned your own business? _____ If Yes, what type_____

Education: ☐ High School ☐ College / Degree _____ ☐ Post-College / Degree _____

Other Special Education or Training _____

Why are you looking for a business opportunity? _____

What is your timeframe to purchase? ☐ Immediate ☐ No hurry

How long have you been looking? _____

Would you work in the business ☐ Full-time ☐ Part-Time

Place a check mark beside each business category that interests you:

☐ Manufacturing	☐ Any Business that can be relocated
☐ Distribution	☐ Retail
☐ Computer/Hi Technology/Sciences	☐ Services: postal, copy centers etc.
☐ Absentee Ownership	☐ Restaurant /Fast Food
☐ Turnaround Situations	☐ Gas Stations/Mini Marts/Car Washes
☐ New or Existing Successful Franchises	☐ Dry Cleaning
☐ Any Business which receives cash payments	☐ Home Based Business

List 3 things that are important to you about any business you might consider buying:

1._____

2._____

3._____

Geographic Location Desire: _____

How far from your home are you willing to drive one way to the business you will buy?

_____

If you reside outside California and have inquired about a California based business, what are your relocation plans and timeframe? _____

Additional information that you think may help us locate a desirable business opportunity for you: _____

FINANCIAL INFORMATION FOR: **Please print name:** _____

(Please attach prepared financial statement, if available)

What is your current annual income? $_____

What are your income expectations the first year of owning your own business?

$_____

Have you ever filed bankruptcy? _____ Had a foreclosure? _____

Had a judgment filed against you? _____

Is there any reason you might be declined a loan for a business acquisition? _____

Will anyone advise you in the review of business records and the decision to purchase any business? _____

What is the down payment amount and the source of funds that you **are prepared to substantiate** at the time of making an offer? $_____

Source: _____

Do you have a financial partner or any other personal source of investment capital?

☐ Yes ☐ No

If Yes, please explain:

_____

Do you have additional income sources? ☐ Yes ☐ No

If yes, please explain: _____

NET WORTH:

ASSETS		LIABILITIES	
Cash in checking accounts	$_____	Notes payable to banks	$_____
Cash in savings accounts	$_____	Notes payable to finance co's	$_____
Stocks and bonds	$_____	Real estate indebtedness	$_____
IRA's, retirement plans, 401K's	$_____	Automobile(s) indebtedness	$_____
Cash surrender of life insurance	$_____	Owing on life insurance	$_____
Real Estate, home	$_____	Charge accounts	$_____
Real Estate, other	$_____	Credit Cards	$_____
Automobile(s)	$_____	Taxes payable	$_____
Your own business	$_____	Other liabilities (describe):	$_____
Appraised collectibles	$_____	_____	$_____
Money due you	$_____	_____	$_____
Other assets (describe):	$_____	_____	$_____
Total:	$_____	Total:	$_____

NET WORTH (total assets minus total liabilities): $_____

TOTAL MONEY AVAILABLE TO INVESTMENT $_____

I certify that the above information is true and correct and acknowledge receipt of a copy of this profile.

_____   _____
Signature   **Date**

Determine Your Interest

After you complete and return the Non Disclosure Agreement AND the seller or his agent has a basic level of comfort you have the ability to buy the business including obtain finance, obtain any necessary licenses and permits and meet other necessities to effectively run the business, you will receive a lot of detail and information about the business. Before you delve too deeply into that material I would recommend you visit the business as a "customer" to get your level of comfort with the location of the business, the surrounding environment, and if you see yourself coming to work as the owner of this business. If you don't feel comfortable, for any reason, do not take your inquiry further.

As part of the above process, do some research on the specific industry of this business. The local library would be able to help you with trade magazines and other material or you can go on-line to see if you can find related material. A great place for information would be the Trade Association that this industry is part of. They probably have a trade magazine or newsletter they would send to you. If you phoned and explained that you were planning on entering their industry they should be more than willing to help you as they would hope that you buy that business and join their trade association. If you want some additional information, in Section Eight of this guide there is a topic on doing research with a trade association to learn about the industry and getting up to speed on businesses operating in that industry.

Another source of information would be asking family and friends if they know somebody in the same or a similar industry. If you can find an existing business owner they may be willing to explain what's happening in the economy and how it's impacting their business. Inside knowledge is a great help. If you decide to talk to somebody in the same industry they will probably want to know which business you are thinking of buying. As you have signed and returned the Non Disclosure Agreement this is something you cannot do. Also, be aware that the business person you are speaking with may be interested in expanding, so if you disclose too much information they may decide to make an offer for the business.

If you have actioned the above steps and still feel good about the business, it's time to look deeper into the confidential material supplied to you.

Review Confidential Business Information

The party representing the seller may use a different strategy depending on the business for sale, instructions from the seller, the sensitive information about the business, and other variables. The process I normally use is to provide the business sensitive material about the business such as a copy of the lease, fixtures, furniture and equipment, profit and loss statements, sellers disclosure statement, list of inventory (if available), franchise agreement (if applicable) etc on a secure website. The secure website allows the buyer to log onto the site 24 hours a day, 7 days a week and review the material which in my case will include photos.

With this information, your job as the buyer is to review the material in a reasonable period of time and inform the broker (or the seller if you are dealing direct with him) if you have further interest in the business. It's also courteous to let these people know if you are not interested in the business. It's up to you whether you want to explain why you are not interested. If you think your feedback would assist the business being sold then that's a positive thing to do. How it is received is up to the other party.

The Confidential business information you have been provided should trigger a number of questions. For the sake of order and clarity, I suggest you write down your questions so you can also record your answers and keep track of what you've asked and the response you've received. For a quick and dirty method, my suggestion would be to break your questions down into the following categories. There is nothing magical about these categories. If you have a better system, then go for it but this method works for me. The main categories are as follows though please make sure you add your own questions:

Management:
Within this section you would ask questions about the role of the owner, key employees, full-time and part-time employees, any owner's family members that may work in the business, how much they are paid, the role they play, and if they will continue after the business has been sold. You could also ask if there is a Business Plan and the status of the lease.

Accounting:
Questions that come to mind here include the accounting software used, who does the book-keeping, handles payroll, and is cash or accrual accounting used, etc.

Operations:
This set of questions would focus on the day to day operations of the business. Hours the business is open, who opens, who closes, are security measures used, is there a training manual, operations manual, are there business-supplied vehicles, and simple questions like asking for a description of a typical day.

Sales and marketing:
Understand if there is a sales and marketing plan, what current methods are used to promote the business, any tracking to see if the sales and marketing works, how much is spent etc. Does the business have a website and is it effective?

Technology:
This section may be overkill for the business you are looking at but if computers are part of the business it's good to understand the role they play, the age of the system, who operates and maintains it, etc.

The goal at this point is to decide if you want to spend further time exploring this business and getting more information. If you choose to move forward, there will be more questions plus now trying to get a feel for the business and the seller to see if you see yourself in his role, and whether you can improve the business and take it to the next level while earning the income you need for you and your family.

End Of Chapter Notes

Use this page to write down notes, ideas and other brainstorming for buying your business.

Make a Deal

"You name the price and I'll name the terms."

Tom West, American Business Broker Icon

Introduction

If the business provides genuine interest, the next important step is to meet with the owner of the business. If the owner is not a working owner, it may be worthwhile meeting with the owner and his manager so your questions can not only cover specifics about the financial, legal, and accounting side of the business but also its operations. The final mix of who does and who doesn't attend the meeting will be decided by the seller and buyer. Some sellers may wish to attend the meeting on their own so they protect confidential information. Some sellers will be completely comfortable with disclosing everything but, as I say, the final decision will be with the seller and buyer.

Meet Seller

The first buyer/seller meeting is an important event. Presumably, neither party has met the other previously so both parties have questions for each other. As the buyer, you will have your own set of questions but don't forget the seller is also working through their list of questions. These could include: Does the buyer really have the financial ability to buy this business? Do they have the education, people skills, business and industry background or ability to learn these things?

Because this is the first meeting a number of things need to be accomplished. Apart from the usual greetings, both parties need to arrive at a level of comfort with the other party so they share as much information as possible. A business is in constant motion working with customers, suppliers, employees, and its normal day to day operation. A lot of sellers prefer to meet after the business is closed and there are no employees around. Sometimes the seller prefers to have an initial meeting away from the business so both parties can get to know each other, then decide if it makes sense to have an on-site inspection. Because it's the sellers business and they know more about the business, its best to work with their requirements so you can build a rapport.

Tour Business

They say that first impressions count and I think this is particularly true when you are looking to buy a business and see it for the first time. If you have a positive impression it will go a long way in determining how you feel about the business and the decisions you make as you move forward.

Because this is the initial time you've seen the business, try not to make the meeting too long. Your goal should be to look around, ask some basic questions and get your own feel for the place. I would not take any photos of the business as that will make the seller nervous. Similarly, I would take brief notes but not take a lot of time writing things down in detail. My suggestion is to keep it simple knowing if things are making sense to you then you can always schedule a second visit. Certainly do not leave the business with unanswered questions but also be comfortable knowing that this is the first of many steps and you will have a lot more questions you need answered.

Do A Gut Check To Analyze Your Interest Level

The specific next step is up to you as the buyer. It may involve scheduling a second or third meeting to ask more questions so you can be satisfied with the business, the current role of the owner and the role you will be playing. The place you want to get to is deciding your level of interest and whether you want to make an offer to buy the business and enter into negotiations.

I think without exception, business owners instinctively collect as much data as they can. This data is then processed and analyzed to make sure there are no unanswered questions, or any details that have not been uncovered. With this being done, the final step is to do a gut check to come up with the answer to one question. That one question is – Will I move forward and make an offer or walk away. If the answer is No – let's walk away there is nothing left to decide but taking action to consider other options.

If the answer to that question is "Yes" – then the emotions come into play with the worrying that something may have been missed or can I trust the people I am dealing with, etc. However, if you decide to move forward and make an offer there is a lot to be done before there are any irreversible actions. In simple terms, the buyer has to make an offer and negotiate this with the business owner. Once both parties accept, due diligence is opened so both parties can ask for and receive confidential material about the other party. Once both parties agree, due diligence is complete, escrow is opened and the legalities are addressed so the business transfers to the buyer with everything in order and the seller receives his money from the transaction.

Make An Offer

If your "gut check" suggests this is the type of business you've been looking for and would now like to make an offer, then the relationship with the seller and his intermediary will move to a different level. If you are doing this on your own or with an intermediary, the first thing to do is recognize that things will get stressful until both the seller and buyer reach agreement on a deal. A little further down in this section we go over some negotiation techniques but it's worth keeping the following in mind when negotiating the purchase of a business.

As you prepare your offer, consider the following:
1. Only make your offer when you have all the information you need. Once you make an offer it is very difficult to keep good faith in the transaction by suggesting the original offer you made was too high because you didn't ask all your questions. If after you've made the offer and it's been accepted and you feel the answers you were given to certain questions was misleading, that's a different matter, but the bottom line is that you should only make an offer when you are ready.
2. Time is of the essence. If you want to buy the business make a genuine offer and keep moving through the transaction. Don't make an offer to "test the waters." Most sellers will only give you one chance; if you blow that chance you may not be considered serious regardless of the reason.
3. Time is also of the essence as the seller may receive another offer from another party. A seller can only sell his business to one person. If another offer is accepted, you can ask for your offer to be considered in a backup position but this is not a pleasant place to. If the original offer falls through and the seller says he will now consider your offer there is always a concern that the first fell through because the buyer found out something they didn't like.
4. Making an offer to buy a business has some unusual components to it. It's invariable that your first offer will not be accepted in its entirety as there are so many variables some of which will be more important to the seller than others and so they will want to negotiate those.

5. Can an offer for a business be verbal? Yes, in theory an offer to buy a business can be verbal but this is far from the norm. An offer to buy a business should always be in writing. As a business broker our Asset Purchase Agreement is 10 pages of 12 point type. It is a long document. The document is very clear with what it covers. The goal of the document is not to favor either party in the transaction but in fact be neutral or at least represent what both parties have agreed to.
6. When the initial offer is made it is done so with a lot of goodwill. That is, the document shows what both parties are willing to accept but subject to many conditions. Some examples include, the buyer may make the offer on condition they can obtain finance from a lender, a lease agreeable to the buyer or, the seller will not open up a business within a specified distance for a specified period of time. Other examples could be the seller providing a certain amount of free training or any number of other conditions.
7. Even after both the seller and buyer have negotiated the offer and now accepted it, a lot has to happen before the business closes escrow and there is a change of possession.

Letter Of Intent, Asset Purchase Agreement Or Stock Offer

If you move forward with an offer there are three ways to do this. The first is with a Letter of Intent, the second is an Asset Purchase Agreement and the third is a Stock offer. In Section Two we discussed the differences between an Asset Purchase Agreement V a Stock offer so you can refer back to that section if you have any questions about that.

A Letter of Intent (LOI) is generally crafted by an attorney representing the buyer. In simple terms its goal is to outline a buyers interest in acquiring the sellers business and it explains what the offer would be provided certain conditions or occurrences were met. If agreement is reached on the deal points it can then be converted into an Asset or Stock sale if that's necessary. A Letter of Intent generally includes both binding and non-binding language. For example, the Letter of Intent will agree that all information provided to the buyer be kept strictly confidential and an agreement to negotiate in good faith.

Generally, a LOI is not accompanied by a non refundable deposit but the seller can choose to negotiate that if that's important to them.

Most business broker transactions are done using an Asset Purchase Agreement. More complex and transactions with a higher selling price may be a Stock sale or use a Letter of Intent. Regardless of which format is used, it should truly reflect what you want to do. When the offer is made, it can also be accompanied by any or all of the following:

1. Copy of the buyer's resume to show he has the professional and management skill to run the business.
2. Copy of the buyer's credit score, especially if the buyer is asking the seller to carry a note.
3. Copy of a bank statement to show the buyer has the ability to make a downpayment in cash.
4. A check that matches the deposit the buyer is willing to make to buy the business.
5. If the buyer has been pre-qualified for an SBA loan, this would also be included.

When the buyer offers an initial check with the offer, not all brokers handle it the same way. Some brokers immediately take the check to an escrow company and deposit the check so it is cleared. The check can then be refunded if the buyer decides not to close the transaction during their due diligence inspection. Other brokers hold the check until the buyer completes their due diligence by signing a form confirming due diligence has now been met. The buyer then issues a second check that the broker then takes to open escrow which he does by depositing the first and second check with the escrow company.

Negotiate If Necessary - Counter Offers

Once the buyer makes an offer it brings into play the need for negotiations. An offer document whether it is a Letter of Intent, Asset Purchase Agreement or Stock sale is normally a complex document. Because of its complexity, it is the exception that the offer from the buyer to the seller is acceptable in its original form. What normally happens is a series of counter offers until both parties are satisfied with the deal. To get through the counter offers, it's all about negotiations.

Negotiations to buy a business are interesting. Both the buyer and the seller put a lot of work into the negotiations, for good reasons, as a lot is at stake. It's worth noting however, that once both parties agree on an initial deal, there may be a need to negotiate the original offer once due diligence is complete as either party will have a lot more information. So the point here is not to negotiate too hard or the deal may fall apart because one party was very tough during the initial negotiations and now things have to be renegotiated again because something new has come to light.

If you are new to negotiations here are 10 suggestions to consider. But remember, the essence of a negotiation is not to get everything you want but everything you can live with.

Ten practical negotiating tips.

1. *Prepare, prepare, prepare.*
One of the first rules of negotiations is to prepare. Some negotiators even say that if you enter into negotiations without proper preparation then you've already lost. In order to avoid losing, start with yourself. Make sure it's clear to you what you really want out of the negotiations. There are many deal points to buying a business. Prioritize the deal points so you are comfortable with what's important to you or something you're prepared to give up in order to successfully close the negotiations. If you can, research the other side to better understand their needs as well as their strengths and weaknesses. Enlist help from experts, such as an accountant, attorney or industry expert.

2. Leave behind your ego.
If you are working with an intermediary to make and present an offer, the intermediary will present the offer for you and explain what's being asked for and why. The other party needs to understand how and why the offer was put together. If the points are reasonable they can accept them or provide a counter offer that doesn't discount the importance of the point. If you are working direct with the seller, it's not important who gets credit for a successful deal. The ultimate goal is to make sure the other side feels like the final agreement was more than reasonable and everyone's opinions and needs have been heard.

3. Ramp up your listening skills.
A lot of negotiations seem to include a lot of noise. Blustering, positioning, to-and-froing are negotiation tactics but one of the best ones is saying nothing at all but just listening. If there is ego involved, there will be plenty of talking. The best strategy in this situation is quiet listening while the other party talks and thinks what they are saying is important, and well worth listening to. Encourage the other side to talk first. Don't interrupt. That then helps set up one of negotiation's oldest maxims: Whoever mentions numbers first, loses. While that's not always true, it's generally better to sit tight and let the other side go first. Even if they don't mention numbers, it gives you a chance to ask what they are thinking.

4. If it's important to you – ask.

Another good rule of negotiating is "State what you want – clearly." Too many times in negotiations I see one party very confused about what the other party is asking for. So clarity is key. In a similar vein, when buying a business, allow a reasonable time for the other party to respond and don't make ultimatums.

5. Expect compromise.

When negotiating to buy (or sell) a business, there are many components to the transaction so you should expect compromise and concessions. Part of the strategy is to work out what's important to you, prioritize some sort of order to arrive at your "Walk away" position. A "Walk away" position means you will not move forward with the deal unless you get the following.

6. Offer and expect commitment.

For negotiations to be successful it must have "good faith" from both parties. "Good faith" means doing what you say you will do. Making an offer to buy a business and the subsequent negotiations that eventually lead to a close in the sale generally take anywhere from 45 to 90 days depending on the complexity of the transaction. If you feel the seller is not genuine in their interest to sell, ask that specific question specifically, and then determine your next course of action based on the response.

7. Their problem is not your problem.

During some negotiations the other side will explain in great detail why they can or cannot agree on something. Negotiations are about coming to an agreement when two parties have a difference but it doesn't mean accepting or buying into the party's problem(s). The best solution is to try and solve the other party's problem so it goes away, but this cannot come at too much expense otherwise a new set of negotiations needs to take place.

8. Stick to your values.

The best negotiations are done from a position of values and principles. Integrity is generally not negotiable so if you have a set of guiding principles, stick to them as the other party will think more highly of you than if you compromise. If you find the deal is crossing those boundaries it's a deal you can live without.

9. Pay attention to timing.

An important aspect in all negotiations is timing. Be sensitive about **when** you ask and how long to wait for a reply. Negotiations to buy a business over a weekend or holiday can be difficult as this is personal time. What holidays you observe may not be the same holidays for the other party. Be careful about pushing too hard for a response as a lack of sensitivity may damage what will generally be an extended period of time that the buyer and seller work together.

10. Close with confirmation.

A useful strategy with all negotiations is to conclude the meeting with a summary of the agreements as well as a summary on what was not agreed upon AND whose responsibility it is to work through each point where there wasn't an agreement, and who will be the first to communicate with the other party about it. Make sure everyone agrees at the end of the meeting and quickly follow up in writing be it as a fax or email on all the points.

End Of Chapter Notes

Use this page to write down notes, ideas and other brainstorming for buying your business.

Close the Deal

"It ain't over till it's over."

Yogi Bera

Introduction

If you have come to this stage in the transaction, hopefully you have made a signed offer to the seller that has been negotiated and accepted. If this is the case, you are now ready to do your due diligence. The primary purpose of due diligence is to allow you, the buyer, and your advisors the opportunity to inspect all the documents and supporting information to verify the different representations made by the seller for their accuracy.

In my experience as a business broker and in talking to colleagues, we estimate that 50% of all deals collapse during the due diligence process. The reasons this happens are many and interestingly come from both the seller and the buyer. The reasons may include:

- ✓ The seller is no longer motivated to sell.
- ✓ The seller is not honest about their business and/or their situation. For example, a new competitor is entering the market or the rent is too high making the business unviable or the financial statements do not correspond to what the seller says, etc.
- ✓ Lack of due diligence by the seller. After accepting an offer and talking with their accountant, the seller learns the resulting tax obligations are too high and so they no longer wish to sell.
- ✓ The seller is unwilling to provide some finance by carrying a note.
- ✓ The buyer gets cold feet.
- ✓ The buyer is unable to get finance.
- ✓ The buyer doesn't believe what the seller is representing.
- ✓ The buyer spoke to a "family expert" or "friend" who said that it wasn't a good idea to buy a business.

There is no hard and fast rule, but the due diligence period should take anywhere from one to three weeks, with about two weeks being the norm. Be patient as there is a lot to work through and get right.

Role of the parties

If the seller has been using a business broker to assist with the sale, it is important that they be the conduit between both parties. It is your right, as the buyer, to ask for any information that relates to the operation of the business and to ask questions about the financial information. Make sure you bring your own professionals, such as an accountant, to review the books.

Open Due Diligence

Opening Due Diligence happens once both the seller and buyer have reached written agreement on the price and terms of the sale of the business. An agreement can be verbal but I would discourage either party from moving forward with Due Diligence until a written and signed purchase agreement has been signed by both parties. It's interesting to me that when each party verbally agrees on a certain set of criteria, that when that apparently same agreement is put into words there no longer is an agreement.

The purpose of Due Diligence is that it allows both parties to inspect documents that hopefully reflect and support all the verbal discussions between both parties leading up to the signing of the purchase agreement. I would also add that the Due Diligence goes both ways. If the buyer has made claims that the owner has relied upon to sign the purchase agreement and finds the buyer made false claims, they can cancel the agreement or re-negotiate the terms. Generally, however, the buyer is using Due Diligence to verify the claims of the seller and work out their next steps with some of the terms of the purchase agreement. These next steps could involve talking with the landlord about the lease, working with the lender to continue the loan approval process, working with the franchisor if a franchisee is involved, etc. This is also the time to use your professional team members such as an accountant to check the financial statements of the seller.

A good agreement should detail what the buyer wants to see as well as what the seller wants. It should also require the buyer to provide proof that he/she has a cash down payment to open escrow once Due Diligence is complete, plus a copy of the buyer's credit score and personal disclosure if the offer is subject to the buyer obtaining a loan, or the seller is being asked to carry a note.

A comprehensive checklist is provided over the next three pages. The list is extensive so not all items will apply to your situation. You may need to add your own items as they relate to your transaction, but the checklist should give you a great start. Also, be sure to make a list of any items you would like the buyer to disclose to you.

Write down questions you have about the due diligence process.

Due Diligence Checklist

Organizational Matters

1. Articles of Incorporation amendments/restatements
2. Bylaws/amendments
3. Current domestic stock statement or equivalent
4. Stock transfers ledger
5. Buy-Sell agreements/shareholder agreements
6. Stock restriction agreements
7. Voting Trusts
8. Oral understandings regarding any of the above

Title/Lease Asset Documents

9. Real property deeds
10. List/description of real properties owned
11. Real property leases
12. List/description of real properties occupied
13. List/description of general assets (by type)
14. Bills of Sale/or invoices for equipment and/or inventory stock in trade
15. Automobile and truck registrations
16. List/description of automobiles and trucks owned
17. Automobile and truck leases
18. List/description of automobile and trucks leased
19. Other vehicle/vessels/rolling equipment or machinery leases
20. List/description of other vehicle/vessels/rolling equipment or machinery
21. Office equipment leases (telephone, copy machines, etc.)
22. List/description of office equipment leased
23. Industrial equipment leases
24. List/description of industrial equipment leased
25. Furniture leases
26. List/description of furniture
27. Patent/trademark/service mark registrations
28. List/description of patents, trademarks and service marks
29. Bill of Landing for inventory stock in trade
30. List/description of inventory/stock in trade (type, item and location)
31. List/description of raw materials on hand
32. List/description of raw materials on order
33. Other leases or use agreements not mentioned above
34. List/description of all other assets not mentioned above

Encumbrances

35. Trust deeds
36. Security agreements
37. UCC-1 finance statements
38. Stock pledge agreements
39. Loan documents (including applications)
40. Notes made or held by the company
41. Line of credit agreements
42. Guarantees (company and personal)
43. Notices of default
44. Oral understandings regarding any of the foregoing

Licenses/Permits

45. City business licenses/permits
46. City industrial/occupational permits
47. State industrial/occupational permits
48. State licenses/permits

49. Federal licenses/permits (FCC, etc)
50. Correspondences to/from any state or federal body governing the business or operations of the company

Business Contracts

51. License agreements
52. Royalty agreements
53. Patent/trademark/service mark assignments
54. Dealership agreements
55. Distributorship agreements
56. Vendor agreements
57. Supplier agreements
58. Consulting agreements
59. Employment agreements
60. Independent contractor agreements
61. Asset sale/purchase agreements
62. Employee stock sale/purchase agreements
63. Employee stock subscription agreements
64. Employee stock option plans
65. Employee stock option agreements
66. Pension/profit sharing trust or agreements
67. Medical/reimbursement plans, agreements
68. Trust indentures
69. Oral understandings regarding any of the foregoing

Litigation/Adverse Claims

70. Plaintiff suits – pleadings, discovery, etc
71. Defendant suits – pleadings, discovery, etc
72. Attorney audit response letters
73. Demand letters received/sent
74. Labor board proceeding documents

75. Administrative court proceeding documents
76. Notices of default received
77. Foreclosure/private sale documents
78. Collection letters/dunning letters utilized (form or otherwise)
79. Collection letters/dunning letters received
80. Bankruptcy filing documents

Financial/Tax

81. Three (3) years prior state tax returns
82. Three (3) years prior Federal tax returns
83. Franchise tax board suspension review documents
84. Real property tax assessment notices/documents
85. Personal property/business equipment tax assessment notices/documents
86. Three (3) years prior financial statements
87. Interim financial statements
88. Tax delinquency notices
89. Audit inquiry response letters
90. Summary of all deposit accounts, savings accounts and other accounts
91. Six (6) month prior bank statements (all accounts)
92. Daily check registers/account books (including computer stored information)
93. General ledger books (including computer stored information)
94. Special account ledge books
95. Chart of accounts
96. Daily/weekly chronological financial records.
97. Copy of credit reference materials provided by vendors, etc
98. List of company credit cards and holders

99. List of vendors supplying company on account (with balances and A/R aging)
100. Ledgers showing company A/R with aging
101. Ledgers showing company A/P with aging

Securities

102. State securities permits/notices/filings
103. State securities registrations/ qualifications
104. Federal securities registration/offering circulars/disclosure documents
105. Federal securities compliance documents (10K, 10Q, etc.)
106. Correspondence to/from the New York department of corporations
107. Correspondence to/from the SEC
108. Correspondence to/from any foreign body governing securities matters

General

109. Attorney retainer letters/ correspondence
110. Attorney opinion letter prepared with regard to the company
111. Accountant retainer letter/ correspondence
112. Accountant "working papers" pertaining to previous three (3) years financial statements
113. Insurance policies including business liabilities, disability, medical and workers compensation policies
114. Detail of key management employees: names, addresses, ages, work experience, positions held, job description, salary and benefits

115. General information regarding employees: number of employees (full-time and part-time) by each location and department, percentage of employees who have left company and reasons for departure, working hours and wage levels by position and department
116. Past history of labor problems
117. Details of employees benefits (pensions, bonuses, retirement plans, etc.)
118. Policy manuals or materials
119. Company operational or procedure manuals or materials
120. Employee manuals or materials
121. Employment applications and hiring forms, documents or materials
122. Employment disclosure documents
123. Past and present business plans for company
124. Full organizational chart of company
125. Details of internal operational structures including identity of who plans, checks and carries out functions, who reviews their results, and how the foregoing is accomplished:
a. Management structure
b. Marketing structure
c. Purchasing structure
d. Merchandising structure
126. Particular details of marketing/sales structures, methods and programs, including identity and functions of sales personnel, special or unusual promotional activities, occasional programs and other special sales efforts
127. Materials or substantial contracts of agreements (written or oral) not listed above or otherwise disclosed

Secure Finance

With all the items on the checklist to take care of, often a key component of the deal is the buyer securing financing.

For the lender to accept a request from the buyer to apply for a loan, the buyer will need:
- ✓ An application form from the lender that the buyer needs to complete
- ✓ Proof of the required down payment in cash (and possible supporting document to show where the deposit comes from such as savings or a gift from a family member).
- ✓ A minimum credit score acceptable to the lender
- ✓ Buyer supporting documents for the loan such as tax returns, payroll stubs to show previous wages and income, business plan, confirmation that the landlord is prepared to assign the lease to the buyer, plus other documents the lender will detail as it relates to the specific transaction.

Securing a loan can be a delaying and detailed process. If the business has been pre-qualified for a loan, then using a football analogy, you have moved to the seller's 20 yard line. If the buyer completes the application and receives a pre-qualification letter from the bank, both parties move to the 50 yard line.

The next step is to get a pre-approval letter that says the lender likes the business and likes the buyer for the business, moving the action to the buyer's 20 yard line. The next play is to complete due diligence, get lender instructions and get to the 10 yard line. Now the final play is to open escrow, dot the I's and T's, and run the ball into the end zone for a touchdown by completing the transaction—with everyone celebrating.

Write down questions about the financing process so you can check later.

Obtain Lender Instructions

As we just mentioned, when third party financing is involved, the lender will require a lot of documents. While most of these are provided by the buyer, the seller is also required to provide some documentation. As the process continues, the lender may request even more documents and more information. As the owner of the business, be patient with the process and supply all documents as quickly and readily as you can so the process keeps moving.

If a third party lender provides financing, the time to process all the paperwork and get approval can take anywhere from 30 to 60 days, with 45 days being about the norm. If the third party lender is a loan from the Small Business Administration, there are strict processes for the lender to follow with no shortcuts allowed. Bottom line: Respond as quickly and professionally as you can, otherwise you may end up killing the transaction.

Track requests you receive for lender documents:

Close Due Diligence And Open Escrow

The escrow process is not the same in all fifty US States. In some states an attorney provides the escrow service and may be known as a "transaction attorney." In some states, like California, there are companies that specialize in offering escrow services just like the escrow service when you buy and sell a residential property, but their focus is on commercial transactions.

What does the escrow company do?

1. Serves as a neutral party in the transaction. Their role includes a communication link between all parties in the transaction including seller, buyer, franchisor, landlord, business broker, lending institution, etc.
2. Prepares escrow instructions and amendments.
3. Requests publication, recording and UCC lien searches.
4. Complies with third party lender requirements.
5. Requests a beneficiary statement if the buyer is taking over a debt or other obligation.
6. Receives purchase funds from the buyer and holds them in trust.
7. Pro-rates taxes, interest, rents, and reimburse the seller for their lease security deposit.
8. Secures release of all contingencies or other conditions that are part of the transaction.
9. Closes escrow when all instructions of the buyer and seller have been executed including:
    a. Bill of Sale
    b. Assignment of Lease, sub-lease or new lease
    c. Abandonment of Fictitious Business Name
    d. Clearances from State Board of Equalization, Employment Development Department and Franchise Tax Board (or the equivalent in each state).
10. Disburses funds as authorized by instructions and prepares a statement showing how funds were dispersed.
11. Records UCC-1 and UCC-3, if necessary.

If you have questions about the escrow process, write them down to research further:

Lease – New, Assign Or Sub-lease

If the business has a commercial lease that the buyer wishes to use as part of the purchase this should be one of the first items the buyer and seller start to action once the Due Diligence is complete. The number one reason that a transaction between a buyer and a seller fails to close is that the seller, buyer, and landlord are unable to come to terms on the lease. The help of a professional such as an attorney representing the buyer or the seller may be necessary.

In simple terms, prior to the buyer agreeing to buy the business from the seller, the seller and the landlord has a lease in place. If this document has been executed correctly and there are no outstanding issues, then the document is binding between the seller and the landlord. A lease normally includes a section that states if the seller can assign or sub-lease the space he is leasing to another party.

If the buyer wants to buy the business and continue operations from the same location, the buyer essentially has three options. First, with the permission of the seller, he can approach the landlord and ask for a new lease for a specific period of time. If the buyer is getting an SBA loan, the SBA lender will generally require the buyer to obtain a lease that's at least equal to the duration of the loan. For example, if the buyer wants a 10 year loan the SBA lender is looking for the buyer to get a lease for 10 years. The 10 years can be broken down into an initial 5 year lease followed by a 5 year option.

Second, the buyer with the agreement of the seller and the landlord can take over the existing lease of the seller if the lease includes a provision for it to be assigned. This can be more difficult than it sounds. It would be normal for the seller to approach the landlord to make the request. Depending on the relationship between the seller and the landlord, the seller may initially go on his own or he may take the buyer with him to introduce them, or if a business broker is involved, they may work with the landlord. If the lease only has a short period of time to run before it expires, there are a number of variables. Generally the buyer would want to negotiate a lease that has at least 5 years to run and include say one or two 5 year options. The seller no longer wants any liability with the lease while the landlord may try to keep the seller on the lease in case the buyer defaults on making the rent payments, and so the landlord can then look to the seller for that relief. An additional complication is what was mentioned above. If the SBA lender requires the lease to correspond to the term of the loan, then that needs to happen or the transaction will not close. If the lease has a reasonable length of time before it expires, then this can make it difficult for the seller as the landlord may refuse to let the seller off the lease until their term expires.

Third, some leases have both an assignment and sub-lease provision. A sub-lease allows the seller of the business to contractually lease the space to the buyer. Under this scenario, the buyer pays the rent to the seller who in turn pays the landlord. Subleasing can get very complicated and will be allowed or disallowed depending on each individual transaction and the goodwill of the lender, landlord, seller, and buyer. As the buyer, if your only option is moving into a sub-lease, make sure it works for your lender.

License Requirements – Franchisor/Liquor etc

This topic is a reminder that the transaction to close escrow may require the buyer obtaining a specific license, obtaining approval from the franchisor to transfer the sale of the business or a specific permit such as a Health Department license or gun and ammunition license from the local county, a contractor's license or other necessary legal approval. If this is not done in a timely manner it may delay the transaction closing escrow as it may affect other parts of the transaction, for example, the lender may not agree to release funds until these items are in place.

Start The Bulk Sale Process

If the business is being sold under an Asset Purchase Agreement or all the assets of the business are being purchased by the buyer, then the escrow company may want to execute the Bulk Sale requirements. If the business is being sold as a Stock Sale, this is not required.

Business transactions are considered personal property and are governed under the Uniform Commercial Code (or UCC) that came into effect to synchronize commercial transactions within the 50 States. This was deemed a legal necessity from earlier times as more and more business was done outside each state. For example, a company could buy a product from a company in state A for use in a manufacturing plant in state B. The final product is then warehoused in state C but sold from state D for final delivery to state E. Once again, different states have different processes and different names for it, but the purpose is to prevent any funds from being transferred to the seller until the provisions of the state Bulk Sale process have been met.

The bottom line is that the deal can't close until the Bulk Sale requirements are met. Depending on holidays and the lead time required to meet publication deadlines, it will take a minimum of twelve business days which typically equates to about a 21 day period.

At the time of starting the Bulk Sale process, the escrow company will deal with getting state agency releases from states that collect state taxes, employment or wage taxes, state income taxes, local county taxes, etc. They will also perform searches to make sure there are no loans, leases, liens or judgments that affect the personal property or assets of the business being transferred to the buyer.

If you have questions about the Bulk Sale process, write them down here:

Purchase Price Allocation

One item that needs to be addressed prior to closing escrow is the Purchase Price Allocation. This is a statement from both the seller and the buyer describing how the total purchase price will be broken down for tax reporting purposes. There may also be other implications. For example, in California, sales tax needs to be paid on the fixtures, furniture, and equipment. If the current rate is 7.75% and the value of the FF&E is agreed at $100,000, the buyer will need to pay $7,750.00 in sales tax—a hidden cost most buyers don't anticipate when starting their journey to buy a business.

Can agreeing with the buyer on how to allocate the purchase price kill the deal? Absolutely! However, we are now in escrow and need to make that final allocation. Hopefully it has been discussed by the seller and the buyer prior to this point so both parties are in agreement, but it is decision time so it needs to be dealt with now.

Write down the Purchase Price Allocation if this is yet to be done.

Sign Final Documents – Close Escrow

One of the deal points that came with the initial offer and was either negotiated or accepted was the date to close escrow and the Change of Possession.

Closing escrow generally requires the buyer and seller coming together on the agreed date and respectively signing the final paperwork. If the business includes inventory, there should have been a final count of the inventory conducted by either parties or an independent third party. Regardless, both parties need to sign a document agreeing on the final value of the inventory.

Along with the signing for the inventory, the buyer needs to inspect all the Fixtures, Furniture and Equipment to agree it is in operational order and is all present and accounted for. Any discrepancies could prevent the closing of escrow or a last minute negotiation to compensate the buyer on the missing or inoperable item.

In Northern California it is customary to use an escrow company to handle the close of the transaction. Other methods include using a transaction attorney whose responsibility is to represent the transaction so the deal is closed. A transaction attorney does not give each party legal advice. They would obtain this from their own attorney.

Hopefully closing escrow and Change of Possession are the same day but it does happen where paperwork is yet to be completed be it from a third party lender or a missing signature on a legal document that theoretically prevents the business from officially transferring from the seller to the buyer.

If this situation arises the owner of the business has a decision to make. That decision is whether he lets the buyer start running the business or waits until the problem preventing escrow closing is fixed. Each situation is unique so it will be a matter for the owner to decide. Under normal circumstances, I don't allow the buyer to take ownership of a business, as once what is happening is announced to suppliers, customers and employees, as they say, you cannot "unring the bell".

Create Your Legal Entity

If all the details are in order, both parties sign closing documents and the business now changes possession, as the buyer of the business you want to make sure your legal entity is in operation so you can bring the assets of your purchase into your business. Hopefully you have spent time with your accountant and attorney agreeing on the best legal entity for you to operate.

End Of Chapter Notes

Use this page to write down notes, ideas and other brainstorming for buying your business.

Your First 100 Days

> *"The critical ingredient is to get off your butt and do something. It's as simple as that. A lot of people have ideas, but there are few who decide to do something about them now. Not tomorrow. Not next week. But today. The true Entrepreneur is a doer, not a dreamer."*
>
> *Nolan Bushnell, American Businessman, Founder of Atari Computer*

Introduction

At the conclusion of Section Six we closed escrow and so, as the buyer of the business, you are now the new owner. Congratulations!

The typical buyer moves into the negotiated training period with the seller (and/or the franchise, if this applies.) My hope for you as the owner of your new business is that you quickly build deep foundations so your business operates successfully for you. To offer some thoughts on how best to do this, the following topics may be of interest to you. Before we get too deep though, you've just taken ownership of your new business, so one of the things you need to decide is whether or not you will do a Grand Opening.

Grand Opening

If you're the new owner of a business and opening the doors for the first time as new owners, it's a big event. This doesn't matter if your business is online, alongside a major freeway or tucked away in a remote industrial or commercial site. Your opening is cause for celebration because of all the work you've done getting to this point plus you need to introduce yourselves business to the world as the new owners of the business.

Hopefully you have been putting together your Business Plan (we'll cover that more in the next topic), and start up budget, and hopefully it has included money to spend on your grand opening. Put planning, money, and energy into creating as much profile as you can. Ideas include:

- ✓ Ask everybody you've sought help or advice from to attend.
- ✓ Consider having the event catered so you can focus on meeting those that attend.
- ✓ Try to tie whatever you're doing with the business you're opening. If it's a food business, prepare and serve as much food as possible. If it's a printing business, hand out plenty of samples and a cross section of work to show what you do. Be creative to gain profile.
- ✓ Use invitations with an RSVP to invite as many people as possible.
- ✓ Decorate the location you will operate from so potential customers in the area now know you are open. If you are in a strip mall invite the other businesses.
- ✓ Consider partnering with other businesses that would benefit from your business. For example, a paper merchant with a printing business.
- ✓ Contact your suppliers you will be buying things from to see if they can give you free items or heavily discounted items you can use to gain visibility of your business.
- ✓ Consider a theme that complements your business. If it's a travel agency and its summer dress in Hawaiian attire.
- ✓ Consider formal invitations if that relates to the type of business you are opening.
- ✓ Contact your local media to see if they will promote your opening. A new business is a positive news story.
- ✓ Invite local business people you haven't met but would like to meet.
- ✓ Invite all your family and friends so you can say thank you to them for their help, but also have as many people attend as possible.
- ✓ Ask your family and friends to bring their family and friends. The more the merrier.
- ✓ Consider as many door prize(s) as possible so as many people as possible remember going to your new business location positively.
- ✓ Use music to add to the event. Try to relate the music to your type of business.

- ✓ If it's a family type business, have something for the children to do and make sure you advertise this so families know they are welcome and treat it as a night out for all their family.
- ✓ Give everybody enough notice so they can plan to attend. A week's notice isn't long enough – 4 weeks is more appropriate – even longer. The longer your time the more people will talk about it and remember your business is now open.
- ✓ Don't worry about timing the Grand Opening to being the first day you open. In fact, consider a "soft" opening where you charge prices so you can "test" everything you do and iron out the wrinkles. Your Grand Opening can then be used to go to your normal prices.
- ✓ Your Grand Opening can go over a weekend or a week or a month. It doesn't need to be one day. If it goes longer than a weekend try to have different things happen at different times so customers come back and build the habit of coming to your business instead of to one of your competitors.

Use this template to jot down things you can do to announce your new ownership of your business. Allocate a cost so you can manage how much you spend.

Business Plan

This is one of the smallest topics in this guide but probably the most important. In my opinion, one of the most important things a business owner needs to do (especially a new business owner) is write a business plan and create a budget and review both documents periodically. The business plan becomes the road map for the new business owner as it forces questions which therefore create or force answers. It's through both the questions and answers you will be able to determine the best direction for your new business.

Not everyone will agree this is the way to go, but it's easy to see if this makes sense by looking at the questions below. All these questions should be typical to most business plans. And that's one of the points. Each business will have things that are unique to its business so a good plan has to be flexible. You can start with a core document and then simply add or remove items as they apply to your business and make sense to you. And remember, one of the best things about a business plan is that it records where you are at, at a certain moment. A business plan is a living and breathing document and needs to be revisited and updated so it stays fresh but keeps you focused and accountable on what needs to be done in the short term and what can and should be moved into the long term.

Within a good business plan is a good budget that also keeps you focused and accountable. If the business is doing better than expected you can ramp up the growth strategy you devised for the business. If the business is not growing as fast as anticipated, you can see the weaknesses and implement solutions to turn things around.

Most business plans have complementary documents attached to it. For example, a good business plan also needs a good Sales and Marketing plan and finance document, which we talk about a little further in this topic. Plus, I suggest you have an additional document called a Productivity Plan. The Business Plan defines the strategic direction of the business, the Sales and Marketing Plan how it sells your product or service, and the Productivity Plan provides a tactical breakdown of steps to take so it all comes together with the success of the business.

Which Business Plan do I use?

There are many software programs available that have different Business Plan templates. Simply search the web and choose the one that works for you. The best news is that they are free. There are a couple of alternatives. First, go to my website http://www.Andrew-Rogerson.com. Once this page loads, on the left hand side there is a menu of options. Towards the bottom there is one called 'Sample Documents.' Click on this option and once this page displays you will see different Word and Excel files. Document #7 is a Business Plan for a start up business while document #8 is a Business Plan for an established business. Both files are documents created by SCORE. There are also other documents on my website that you are welcome to download and use.

The second alternative is to discuss this with your business broker or consultant and see what they use. They may have an option to share with you and if you follow this option and have questions about how to get it completed, they could readily assist you with that.

The third alternative is to create your own from the suggestion below. A complete business plan can range from 10-100 pages. Your plan should be a work in progress so be sure to write it using a word processing system so you can make changes and update it over time.

Sample Business Plan

I. Company Description/Overview

   A. Nature of Business

       1. Individuals being served/their needs
       2. Why your area?

   B. Your Distinctive Competencies (primary factors that will lead to your success)

       1. Superior customer need satisfaction
       2. Production/service delivery efficiencies
       3. Personnel
       4. Geographic location

II. Market Analysis

   A. Target Markets

       1. Demographics
       2. Geographic location
       3. Seasonal/cyclical trends

   B. Competition

       1. Identification
       2. Strengths (competitive advantages)
       3. Weaknesses (competitive disadvantages)

III. Products and Services

   A. Detailed Product/Service Description (from the user's perspective)

       1. Specific benefits of product/service
       2. Ability to meet needs
       3. Competitive advantages

IV. Marketing and Sales Activities

   A. Overall Market Strategy

       1. Market penetration strategy
          a. Intended means (including advertising, promotion, printed matter, etc.).
       2. Growth Strategy

V. *Management and Ownership*

    A. Management Staff Structure

    B. Key Managers (including self)

          1. Name
          2. Position
          3. Primary responsibilities and authority
          4. Primary responsibilities and authority with previous employers
          5. Unique skills and experiences that add to your company's distinctive competencies

    C. Legal Structure of the Business

VI. *Organization and Personnel*

    A. Recruitment procedures
    B. Staffing levels

8 Important Functions Of A Business Plan

Most small business owners and future entrepreneurs have probably read and heard how it is important to have a business plan. As I travel through my world as a business broker I am surprised to see that very few business owners actually have one, or if they have it, rarely look at it and pay attention to it. If finance is required to grow the business, the business owner puts together a business plan, secures the finance, and promptly forgets about it. You may not realize, however, the benefits of a business plan expand well beyond that single use. It is also a critical tool for your use as you develop and grow your business and here's why.

The business plan is a written document that clearly identifies and defines the goals of a business and precisely outlines the methods for achieving them. It provides a complete and detailed description of how the business will operate and just as importantly, a communications tool not only for investors but also the key management of the business, and others interested in understanding the operations and goals of your business. Your business plan is a living and breathing document and a blueprint on how you are going to build your company. Here are 8 important functions of your business plan:

1. A road map for your initial crucial startup decisions.

It is a management and financial "road map." In short, it is your most important guide to starting, building, and managing a successful business.

2. The place to clarify your ideas and plan of action.

It explains how the business will function in the marketplace. It describes what you are selling, your background and qualifications, who your prospective customers are, where they can be found, what is needed to build the business, how you plan to promote, and determine the viability of the venture in a designated market.

3. It is an operational tool.

The business plan is a tool that clearly depicts characteristics which, when properly used, will help you manage your business and work toward its success. It is a means for communicating your ideas to others by measuring operational progress.

4. A financial tool.

By determining how much money will be needed for start-up costs, it details how the business will be financed. And, as a prospectus for potential investors, it is an important tool to help obtain financing by anticipating ongoing capital and cash requirements to reassure lenders or backers.

5. Place to benchmark and establish best practices.

The finished business plan will be a strategic operational tool that complements the sales and marketing plan and tactical productivity plan to provide guidance to the entrepreneur in organizing planning activities to help move the business forward. A business plan is all about the business, its goals, and its road map to achieving those goals.

6. Future growth.

This is the place to explain how you plan to keep your business growing. It is a detailed guide of what you are going to do and how you are going to increase your profits. These plans should outline your specific goals for the coming one, two, and three years. By breaking your objectives down into quarterly, semi-annual, and annual milestones, your plan will give you foundations and roots to provide a realistic determinant of your ultimate success. If your Business Plan is still a work in progress or been neglected for more than one quarter, now is the time. Your company's success depends on it!

7. A place to record goals and metrics for accountability.

A business plan is a place to write down short term and long term goals and hold all stakeholders accountable in reaching those goals. If it is written down and you choose to walk away from agreements or milestones, you do so at the peril of the business failing.

8. A place to be honest.

This may sound simplistic, but it's the place to be honest. You can write things down in a business plan and then forget about it. What a waste of time. Or you can embrace the Business Plan and what it stands for, and regularly check you are executing the strategy that everyone bought into and thereby keep not only your team, but also you, focused.

Importance of your Business Plan

If the above section on the importance of a business plan makes sense to you, it will have more meaning as you work with and create your own business plan. A business plan forces discipline and accountability, which is what a business is all about. It allows you to be creative and write down what you are thinking so you can come back to it at any time and see if you are going in the direction you planned. If you've wandered off track, the business plan will allow you to see that and re-focus.

In my opinion, the number one reason for creating a business plan is that it works with your sales and marketing plan and productivity plan. The business plan covers strategic goals and vision, the sales and marketing plan is the what, where, when, and how to achieve the goals of the business. The productivity plan is a blend of the business and sales and marketing plan by breaking down into tasks and responsibilities what needs to be done on a daily and weekly basis.

The biggest complaint I hear about a business plan is that you have to keep it up to date. Absolutely – that's its primary purpose. If your business plan is out of date it means you have started in a different direction than you planned. But it means your business plan must be brought up to date so you are forced to consider the direction you are drifting in case that direction is wrong.

Finally, as the owner of the business, you own your Business Plan. If it doesn't work for you it won't work for anybody else. It's as simple as that!

Sales And Marketing Plan

If you would like to create a sales and marketing plan and put it in writing, below is a suggested outline. The main strategy to follow is to have the Sales and Marketing Plan work in conjunction with the Business Plan and the Productivity Plan (which we will talk about shortly.) I do think it's a great idea to put your plan into a written document as this process makes you focus and work through the variables. Plus once it's written down it's so easy to go back and review it and make changes as necessary.

Sales and Marketing Plan outline:
1. Executive Summary

The easiest strategy for creating the Executive Summary is to simply take it from the business plan. It can also be a fresh document, the choice is yours.

a. Description of the Company
The company description includes a brief history such as when it was founded, and general information about the current owners of the business. Keep it simple and to about 10 lines.

b. Vision Statement
If the company has one, simply place it here. A good vision statement shouldn't need explanation. A very brief history about how the vision statement was chosen can be included, if necessary.

c. Mission Statement
Same as the Vision Statement. Drop it in here and move on. The mission statement should be included on all marketing plans.

d. Products and Services
A very brief description of the company's products and services. If the sales and marketing plan is internal and won't go to a lender or used by another company unfamiliar with the business then no detailed explanation is required. If this document can go to external customers or vendors then a brief explanation of the main products and services is a good idea.

e. Financial Feasibility
This section should also come straight from the business plan and give a brief description of the financial outlook of the industry and the company, and what effects may arise if the marketing is not successful. Don't discuss financial plans for the marketing program in this section of the document.

2. Strategic Focus and Plan

a. Mission/Vision
This is the place to state what you would like out of the marketing plan. If this is a marketing plan for a single product, then this statement should state what your company expects out of the product and how they plan to achieve the goals.

b. Objectives

The objectives of the marketing for the particular product, service or company should be outlined in this section. If one of the objectives is to make 50,000 people aware of your new product then this is something that should be included in your objectives. You can also include company objectives in this section if they are directly affected by your marketing. For instance, if your goal is to make one million dollars in sales the first year, then this is an objective that comes in direct contact with the marketing program.

c. Competitive Environment

Companies don't exist in a vacuum. They have competition. Outline the competitive environment of your product, market or service. This would include any competitors whether they are in direct or indirect competition.

d. Situation Analysis

A good marketing tool that outlines the products and their effectiveness is a SWOT Analysis. SWOT stands for Strengths, Weaknesses, Opportunities, and Threats. On page 154 we show a SWOT template. Review this model and process and include it in your Sales and Marketing report to bring clarity.

e. Competitive Analysis

This section differs from the competitive environment as it describes more in-depth how you plan to effectively market against the competition. This section should outline direct competition's weaknesses, and how you plan to capitalize on these weaknesses to grab the market share.

3. Market Product Focus

a. Marketing Objectives

Your marketing objectives can take one of two formats: strategic or tactical. If the marketing plan is to outline all objectives of the company you would write strategic objectives. You could list these in numerical order and explain in detail how those objectives are to be accomplished. Should the plan be for a specific product or service it would be tactical. Use the same number and descriptive format but instead this time explain the objective and tie it in to the strategic sales and marketing plan so the reader can see what is to be accomplished.

b. Target Markets

All products and services are created to meet the demand of a target market or markets. Use this section to define in detail the market in which you will be marketing your product. Describe in detail the target market(s) and outline your conclusions. Clearly state why this market is going to use your product or service and support your argument with the research that's been done to arrive at this conclusion.

4. Marketing Program

a. Product Strategy

If you are selling a product, outline the strategy you will use for this product with a detailed description of your product(s) are and how they are going to benefit your company. If you are doing an individual product marketing plan, then this section would describe in detail what your product is and what strategies you have to make it beat out your competitors.

b. *Price Strategy*

The price strategy is where you will describe your key pricing issues. It is a good idea to state whether you are taking the high cost/low turnover method or the low cost/high turnover method. If you think your key selling point is going to be the price, then explain that here. If you are taking the low cost/high turnover approach, then explain how your company will succeed with the low profit margin on each product. Be sure to include rough estimates of profit margins, manufacturing costs, and end consumer prices.

c. *Promotion Strategy*

The promotion strategy is one of the most important sections of the marketing plan. This is where it can make or break a marketing program. This section should include advertising strategies you plan to engage in, any marketing strategies for your products such as attending trade shows, conferences etc. Also you should explain what message you want to promote in all of the items mentioned above. You should send the same message through all channels of communication.

Get on with it!!

Now that you have your plan, go out and make it real. There is no use spending months in analysis paralysis trying to write a perfect plan. Rather, have a bias towards action and go get started NOW.

Importance of your sales and marketing plan

The Sales and Marketing plan ties in with the Business Plan and argues the method to attract new customers, keep the existing customers, and thereby grow the business. It also focuses on the product or service(s) you are offering, and what research has been done to support the premise that there is a market for the product, and that market will allow you to build and deploy your product or service and at the end of the day, not only cover your costs but make a profit.

From my perspective, the better the Business Plan, Sales and Marketing Plan, and Productivity Plan are all tied in together with a financial strategy AND communicated to the employees so they understand their role, the more successful the business will be. If the economy is struggling, then the impact may not be obvious but you will be doing things your competitors are not doing. Use these different plans you make to give your business foundation and direction, and success will come to you.

Elevator Speech

So what's an elevator speech? Imagine you walk into the first floor of an elevator and you push the tenth floor button. You see the third floor button's been pushed and so you turn around to see the person and the person you see is one of the most important people you would like to meet. The first thing you would probably think of doing is getting off at the third floor but you've pushed the tenth floor button. So you need to find a way between the first floor and the third floor (about 15 to 30 seconds) to convince that person that they need to spend more time with you, preferably with a second meeting so you can really explain what it is that you have to say. So that's an elevator speech. The ability to convert a first time contact with somebody into a second meeting or appointment by having something specific and universal to say under any situation. In simple terms, you need an advertisement about you and your business to knock their socks off in the shortest time possible.

Critically – make it short, simple and memorable and rehearse it thoroughly so it sounds natural and not contrived.

Sample elevator pitches:

"I'm the owner of an auto body shop in North Highlands called Sam's. It's a new business and if your car breaks down and needs repair we do all the work for you and provide a free rental until it's fixed. I also service all American made cars and guarantee to have the job finished the same day as long as the car is at my business by 8.00 am."

"I'm a business broker and have owned five businesses. All my discussions with you are totally confidential. Before I list a business for sale I do a Brokers Opinion of Value so you can decide if the valuation price is right or not. My cost includes advertising the business on 41 websites and I am only paid if your business successfully sells. My qualifications include being a Certified Business Broker."

> **Write some sample elevator speeches in pencil so you can tweak and change. Once you get the one you like, commit it to memory and practice it in front of a mirror until it becomes natural.**

Productivity Plan

Most business owners are familiar with the idea of a business plan and possibly a sales and marketing plan. Based on my observations, most small business owners don't have a business plan nor indeed a sales and marketing plan. I suspect the reasons include they do not have the time to create the document, see little value in spending the time to start it as they are not sure when they will need it.

The true value of a business plan is that it forces ideas or more specifically, goals, to be written down on paper. As business owners, we carry ideas in our head and because we live and breathe the business think we have its direction under control. I suspect this is far from the truth. As the saying goes, if you fail to plan, you plan to fail.

So here's the solution.

The business plan is the strategic vision and direction of the business. This should be a living and breathing document that is constantly changed. The sales and marketing plan is a subset of the business plan in that it defines how customers are created, kept, and maintained. Again, this should be a living and breathing document. From my perspective, the document missing that truly brings the business plan and sales and marketing plan together is the productivity plan.

A productivity plan is the tasks that need to be completed on either a daily, weekly or monthly basis. These tasks can be divided into basic operations to marketing and sales activities; whatever flows from the business and sales and marketing plans.

Use your plan to get the most out of each work day.

Create your plan

The productivity plan applies at the individual level by defining tasks and goals to achieve. If there are particular tasks you need to complete each week to achieve that goal, designate a specific day of the week to accomplish this task. For example, you might conduct a team meeting on Mondays, schedule one-on-one time with key employees on Tuesdays, review financial statements on Wednesdays, etc.

Assigning important tasks to a specific day of the week will help get you into a routine and minimize distractions or if your productivity plan gets full and the task you need done is important, you can delegate it and schedule a task to review the results with the person you delegated the task. Also, by breaking down tasks, it often creates a sub set of tasks all of which need to be done. For example, if your team meeting is planned for Monday you may need to create a subset of tasks such as getting a report completed by end of business Wednesday, as preparation for a meeting on Thursday with your sales and marketing person, phoning to get quotes on certain items, ordering a new piece of equipment etc and schedule training on it etc so everything is ready for the next weekly Monday meeting.

As you plan your productivity list, before accepting it, try to answer the following questions.

1. Will this task help me with my general organization?
2. Will this task improve the company's bottom line?
3. What tasks should I be doing that I tend to avoid?
4. Is this task part of my responsibilities or can it be delegated or outsourced for a cheaper cost than me doing it?

Here are some other ideas to stimulate your thoughts. These thoughts are sales and marketing centric so you can adapt these to different areas of the business such as management, finance, Human Resources etc.

1. Perform 10 cold calls today
2. Attend Wednesday evening networking event
3. Add a new page to the website or update an existing page
4. Submit an article to the local press
5. Attend a monthly webinar on the latest sales techniques
6. Meet weekly with a mentor
7. Read industry newsletters or magazines etc first thing Thursday morning
8. Speak in public on a monthly basis

Write your plan in either a word processing document or in a spreadsheet format, and update it regularly, preferably on the same computer as your business plan and sales and marketing plan so you can synchronize all of them. You could also consider printing it out and posting it near your desk so it's always handy. In addition to a weekly plan, you can also define monthly and yearly goals. Once you begin to check off tasks, not only will you feel a sense of accomplishment, but your productivity will inevitably improve.

Your plan doesn't have to stop with you. If you have employees or a virtual assistant, be sure to create plans for them too. Soon everyone in your business will be working smarter and your only regret will be that you didn't create your plans sooner.

"The short-term plan, then, is an operative plan of defining goals in writing and clearly indicating how these goals are to be carried out ..."

American Management

Value Of A Mentor

There's a great quote that goes something like this "If I was the sole source of inspiration for my business it would go broke." In very simple terms, one person cannot do it all. There are too many variables, quick and constant change, the need to have balance in our lives.

A solution to the above is to find a mentor. Let me be a little clearer – the solution to the above is to find a good mentor that works for both of you. If you are lucky enough to find the right mentor then it can bring so many positive contributions to what you do.

8 tips to find a good mentor

1. Probably the two most important ingredients in a mentor relationship are integrity and character both couched in someone you respect and trust. Look for integrity and character and if that works, make sure there is respect and trust…in both directions.
2. Possibly the hardest part is finding someone interested in working with you as a mentor. They need to be open and willing to relate and work with you as the relationship should naturally involve discussing both professional and personal issues.
3. If the last point is challenging, the number one reason it can be hard to find the right mentor is that they simply lack the time. Try to find someone who has the time and the willingness to spend with you. This may take time but you'll have to be patient as the mentor relationship you seek is long term for a true mentor relationship to evolve and truly work. Part of your requirement is to be flexible and work in with your mentor's schedule.
4. A good question is whether to look for somebody in your industry or completely removed from it. The best option is to find somebody in the same or a similar industry who is not a competitor as this cuts down a lot of work explaining industry jargon and problems. However, the key is that the relationship works for both parties, so lack of industry knowledge can be overcome if the ingredients are right.
5. Similarly, don't be afraid to look beyond your neck of the woods. A person with an expertise in another discipline or field can provide new insights about different business principles, and provide a new perspective.
6. A word of caution. Your mentor will be human. A good mentor will provide new insights, but they won't solve all your personal or business problems. In fact, a good mentor will help you solve your own problems or if they feel it is necessary, direct you to another source for special problems.
7. Openness is one of the key ingredients to a mentor relationship. If you don't feel comfortable being open and honest with someone, then mentoring is not for you. A good mentor will let you into their world, sharing both professional and personal triumphs and failures.
8. Mentoring is a journey and takes time to evolve. As long as you're learning something you didn't know before, the mentoring relationship is working. Like all good things in life, it takes as long as it takes.

Tax Planning

One of many tasks a business owner needs to manage is the tax consequences that come from the profits of the business. Obviously the business owner needs to withdraw money on a regular basis especially if the profits from the business are the single source of income for the family. However, if the business produces profits that attract high taxes, It's good business to understand the amount of those taxes, when they will be incurred (which tax year), when they need to paid, or more importantly, what can be done to legally minimize or reduce the taxes.

Most business owners don't know the answer to the above questions and more; it is simply outside their expertise. This makes sense too, as the owner of your business your skill and expertise is best focused on what you do best and that is run your business. However, tax planning makes good business sense so let's dig in a little deeper.

If you have an accountant or tax advisor, this is the first place to start. They should already know your business and your personal tax situation so you will be a step ahead. If you use a bookkeeper instead, ask them for their thoughts. If you prepare your own financial statements and tax returns, find a professional and spend the money for a one- to two-hour consultation.

Make the most of your investment by preparing for your meeting before you visit the accountant. Following are some considerations:
- ✓ Are you after a short-term or long-term relationship—and what are they offering?
- ✓ What education qualifications do they have?
- ✓ What are the costs?
- ✓ What is their business expertise?
- ✓ Are you better off looking for an advisor who not only knows small businesses but also the particular industry you work in? For example, if your business is a medical practice, are you better off with a tax advisor who knows that industry and some of the "hidden" tax minimization options?
- ✓ Do they have a code of ethics or belong to any associations that do?
- ✓ Do you know somebody else who has used their services? If not, ask for referrals and visit their website to get more information about them.
- ✓ Can you identify their client base? If so, do you think this is a customer base that is similar to the industry you work in?
- ✓ Would they consider a free initial consultation so you can see if there is a match with the service they provide and what you need?

Finding a Tax Advisor

If you plan on doing your own bookkeeping or using the services of a bookkeeper, you want to do some research to find a professional who can advise you on minimizing your tax liability year in year out.

When looking for a tax advisor, consider answering the following questions so you find the right person for you.

1. How complex do you consider your situation and how much advice do you think you need? (Obviously a tough question but I suggest listing questions/topics below so you can research and find the answers in order to hire the right person for the job.)
2. Are you looking for a short-term engagement to get immediate answers to questions or are you looking for a long-term relationship?
3. Certified Public Accountants (CPA) are qualified to offer more complex business and personal

financial advice. This may be the skill set you need to get the advice you need. Like most things in business, their fee should come with a return on investment.

4. Another option to consider is a Certified Financial Planner as they may be able to suggest tax minimization options as well as ways to invest that money and grow it even more.

Write your tax planning questions you would like to research on your own or with the help of a professional advisor.

End Of Chapter Notes

Use this page to write down notes, ideas and other brainstorming for buying your business.

Additional Information and Tools

"The amount of data and analysis available for free is a true example of information explosion that has leveled the playing field for individual investors."

Maria Bartiromo

Introduction

The following introduces a few different options that may be of interest to a buyer when looking for sources of third party finance. The information could also be given to a seller so they can explore further themselves. Third party finance options are many and varied but here a few highlights.

It is also not unusual for a small business transaction to incorporate a mix of funds. For example, the buyer puts down 15% of the purchase price, the seller carries back 10% and the balance of the purchase price comes from a third party loan from a lender. Like all things in the deal, this is a negotiation.

SBA Program And Other Finance Options

SBA Program

The Small Business Administration (SBA) has a range of loan programs available for qualifying businesses. There are two types of lenders: a Non-Preferred Lender and a Preferred Lender. Finding a Preferred Lender is generally the best option as these lenders are empowered to make credit decisions for the SBA. Preferred Lenders include banks, national lenders such as CIT, and popular small business and regional lenders such as Comerica and PNC.

There are extensive rules and regulations to follow that cover the SBA loan program and the lenders are also subject to conflicts of interest and ethical requirements. For example, it is very difficult for a buyer to borrow funds if they have a federal felony conviction. It is also highly unlikely to obtain a loan approval if it is to buy "a house of ill-repute," as it was called in the old days. Sex may sell but it doesn't mean you can get an SBA loan to borrow money to buy a business that engages in it.

To purchase a small business, the loan is usually either a 7(a) or 504 loan. A 7(a) loan is available to purchase a business between $25,000 and $2,000,000. However, a lot of lenders are not interested in loans under $100,000 due to the high cost of processing and meeting compliance requirements. If real estate is involved, a 504 loan would be used and the deal can go up to $6,000,000 in total finance.

For a buyer to be eligible for an SBA loan they must:
- ✓ Intend to run the business (it must be owner operated, not an investment),
- ✓ Be a US citizen (resident aliens may apply but INS gets involved, taking more time),
- ✓ Be at least 21 years old
- ✓ The business must have cash flow to meet the debt service.

For more information on the SBA programs, visit: http://www.sba.gov or send me an email to info@andrew-rogerson.com so I can connect you with a lender.

Other finance options

BORSA

BORSA stands for Business Owners Retirement Savings Account. This is a tool which allows you to fund the business start up, purchase a franchise or buy business property using your holdings in your 401(a) pension, profit sharing 401(k), 403(b), 457, IRA rollover or Roth IRA. Through the utilization of a BORSA, these purchases can be accomplished without distributions, taxes, penalties or the use of loans.

A leading provider of BORSA programs is DRDA. You can get more information from their website at http://www.drdacpa.com.

Guidant Financial Group

Another source of funds for your business startup that is similar to option one above that is to use the existing funds in your IRA. Guidant Financial Group is able to advise you on how to use a self-directed structure to access your retirement funds.

For more information, visit the Guidant website at http://www.guidantfinancial.com.

SD Cooper

Your 401K or IRA account may be used to fund the startup of a new business. SD Cooper provides a service that allows you to put the right structure in place. For more information, visit their website at http://www.sdcooper.com.

> *"Apply yourself. Get all the education you can get, but then, by God, do something. Don't just stand there, make it happen."*
>
> *Lee Iacocca*

Recasting Financial Statements

Introduction

This section is included for the curious. The explanation and information provided may be considered technical and has been added to provide a reasonable explanation of the term Discretionary Earnings. If you are not interested, read no further.

For a profitable business to sell, it must have an asking or list price. For those that trade on the stock market and are used to prices of stocks, you will be familiar with EBIT and EBITDA terminology. However, when selling a business, the starting point for a valuation is the amount of Discretionary Earnings (DE). This is the methodology used by the International Business Brokers Association and the various affiliated state associations including the California Association of Business Brokers.

Discretionary Earnings are defined as:
- ✓ Net Income Before Taxes,
- ✓ Depreciation and Amortization,
- ✓ Interest,
- ✓ Owner's (one owner) Compensation,
- ✓ IRS Code Section 179 (non-recurring expenses).

From a business valuation perspective, the difference between Discretionary Earnings (DE) and EBITDA is that for public companies it includes the management expense at fair market value, whereas for private companies it includes owner's compensation and perks.

DE does not equal EBITDA—they are completely different and should not be confused. You arrive at DE by recasting the financial statements, that is, Income Statement and/or tax returns and the Balance Sheet. Recasting means taking the numbers from these financial statements and using only the true income and costs needed to run the business.

But why do we need to know the amount of the business Discretionary Earnings?
1. Discretionary Earnings "normalizes" the income the business produces to provide a more accurate picture of the cash available to a buyer and the real value of the assets.
2. Business owners want to minimize their taxes; therefore they claim as many expenses as possible to reduce their taxable income.
3. It provides protection for the buyer. For example, the owner may own the property that is not being sold with the business but has not been expensing an amount for rent. The seller charges $2,000 per month for the lease so this has to be "normalized" into the Discretionary Earnings. Another example is the seller may be using a spouse or friend to "help" in the business but not pay them anything. A buyer needs to replace that free labor at a cost which should be part of the "normal" operating cost of the business.
4. Recasting helps buyers compare "apples with apples."

Instructions

The Discretionary Earnings is the basis for the financial strength and selling price of your business. When buying a privately held company, the buyer will use this number to determine the financial attractiveness of your business when compared to other businesses that are for sale. The buyer will also use this information during due diligence to compare the numbers against the tax return and other financial statements.

On the following page is a blank worksheet and following that, a sample worksheet has been provided for your reference. If you have your tax returns and Profit and Loss statement you can calculate your own Discretionary Earnings.

Here are the steps to follow:
1. Round all numbers to the nearest dollar.
2. Label the headings with the year or period that the column applies. For example, in YTD Current Year add "2008." In the next column show "2007," in the next "2006," or whatever is appropriate.
3. Review lines 5 through 8 and write in these numbers as shown on the tax return.
4. Review lines 11 through 23 and again write in these numbers from the tax return. Add backs are items that the owner or seller has paid through the business but are not true business expenses. They are paid through the business because the business has the cash flow to support it and/or it reduces the owner's taxable income. They lower the value of the business, hence the reason they are added back. The seller must be able to prove these items to the buyer's satisfaction. Add backs are also onetime expenses that reflect unusual or non-recurring expenses a new owner will not be required to pay.
5. Review lines 25 & 26 in case there are adjustments in the favor of the buyer that you need to include.
6. Add together lines 5, 6, 7 & 8 to arrive at a total at Line 9.
7. Now add line 4 plus line 9 plus any amounts shown from line 11 through 23 and deduct any amounts shown at lines 25 & 26 to get a total of Discretionary Earnings.

Remember, Discretionary Earnings are defined as:
- ✓ Net Income Before Taxes,
- ✓ Depreciation and Amortization,
- ✓ Interest,
- ✓ Owner's (one owner) Compensation,
- ✓ IRS Code Section 179 (non-recurring expenses).

		YTD Current Year	20..	20..	20..
1	Sales				
2	Less Cost of Sales or Cost of Goods				
3	Less Total Operating Expenses				
4	**= Net Income or Pretax Profit**				
5	Plus Depreciation				
6	Plus Amortization				
7	Plus Interest				
8	Plus Owners Salary or Draw				
9	**= Adjusted Earnings**				
10	**Add back** the following **(if applicable)**				
11	Plus Payroll Tax Paid on Owners Salary				
12	Plus Benefits Paid to Owner (i.e. Health Ins)				
13	Auto—Owners Personal Expenses				
14	Auto—Owners Insurance				
15	Auto repairs—Owners Personal Expense				
16	Charitable Contributions				
17	Rent—Adjust to Fair Market Rate				
18	Insurance—Owners Personal Health, Life, etc.				
19	Retirement Plans—Owner Paid Contributions				
20	Plus Meals and Entertainment				
21	Plus Travel—non-related business				
22	Plus Telephone and Cell Phone—non business				
23	Plus one time charges (i.e. bad debt, etc.)				
24					
25	**Less the following (If applicable)**				
26	Market Rate for Non-paid Family or Friends				
27	Market Rent if Rent Charged is Below Market				
28					
29					
30	**Total Discretionary Earnings**				

Example

		YTD Current Year	2007	2006	2005
1	Sales		565,000	550000	500,000
2	Less Cost of Sales or Cost of Goods		170,000	165,000	150,000
3	Less Total Operating Expenses		335,000	330,000	300,000
4	**= Net Income or Pretax Profit**		60,000	55,000	50,000
5	Plus Depreciation		20,000	20,000	20,000
6	Plus Amortization		5,000	5,000	5,000
7	Plus Interest		5,000	5,000	5,000
8	Plus Owners Salary or Draw		80,000	77,000	75,000
9	**= Adjusted Earnings**		170,000	162,000	155,000
10	**Add back** the following **(if applicable)**				
11	Plus Payroll Tax Paid on Owners Salary		8,000	7,700	7,500
12	Plus Benefits Paid to Owner (i.e. Health Ins)		2,500	2,000	2,000
13	Auto—Owners Personal Expenses		3,500	3,300	3,000
14	Auto—Owners Insurance		2,200	2,000	2,000
15	Auto repairs—Owners Personal Expense				
16	Charitable Contributions		800	650	500
17	Rent—Adjust to Fair Market Rate				
18	Insurance—Owners Personal Health, Life, etc.		1,200	1,000	1,000
19	Retirement Plans—Owner Paid Contributions		5,500	5,000	5,000
20	Plus Meals and Entertainment		1,500	1,400	1,400
21	Plus Travel—non-related business		3,500	3,000	3,000
22	Plus Telephone and Cell Phone—non business				
23	Plus one time charges (i.e. bad debt, etc.)				
24					
25	**Less** the following (If applicable)				
26	Market Rate for Non-paid Family or Friends		-8,500	-8,250	-8,000
27	Market Rent if Rent Charged is Below Market				
28					
29					
30	**Total Discretionary Earnings**		190,200	179,800	172,400

Final Checklist

On the following page is the beginning of a checklist of items that need to be finalized for the business to change possession from the owner to you, the buyer. The checklist is not exhaustive but should give you a good starting point plus there is room for you to add other items as they relate to the business you are buying.

And by the way, congratulations! If you are reading this part of the guide because your journey has come to this point, then your business is now yours and I wish you nothing but success. Well done!

Description	Start Date	Completion Date	Contact
Purchase agreement negotiated and accepted by both parties.			
Due diligence/validations completed			
All purchase documents signed			
Lender finance applications signed and submitted			
Buyer creates own legal entity if using a Corporation. Also need Fed ID# and fictitious name filing with county office			
Open bank account(s) with checks and deposit slips (bank will need Fed ID# and copy of legal entity if a LLC, Partnership or Corporation)			
Insurance: Worker's Compensation; Business; Vehicles; Life			
Lease of premises applied for (if applicable.)			
Determine bookkeeping method: QuickBooks? Print checks/write checks?			
Set up payroll payment process with a vendor			
Credit card processing application & set up (if applicable.)			
Finalize any equipment leases (and delivery)			
Determine processes to handle cash drawer: money, daily receipts and deposits			

Description	Start Date	Completion Date	Contact
Determine how to transfer business records: hard and soft copies			
Organize utilities: Electricity; telephone; long distance; water; trash/sewer Fire Dept./Health Dept. inspection (if applicable)			
Contact vendors to establish credit and relationship			
Ensure all employees have completed HR requirements such as I-9, W-2's etc.			
Organize business contact phone numbers			
Vehicle title; equipment leases			
Document all employee contacts in case of emergency			
Hire employees (if applicable)			
Set up and document emergency business procedures for employees to follow			
Ensure adequate inventory available (if applicable)			
Apply for business license with your local city office			
Apply for Re-sale permit (sales tax permit) with State Board of Equalization (If applicable.)			
Apply for State Employer ID # (SEIN) with Employee Development Department (EDD)			
Apply and obtain any additional Licenses required for your industry/business.			
Create your Business Plan			
Start on your Sales and Marketing plan			
Create your Productivity Plan			

Associations Of Interest

Trade associations can be a wonderful source of help and information for a business owner just starting out. Not only can you get direct and meaningful industry and market help from the people who work at the association, but also from the members who are business owners like you. And like you they started their business life in your industry not knowing much, so if you find a similar minded person to you (or a number of them) you have access to some wonderful and immediate knowledge.

A lot of associations publish a newsletter that offers industry resources and informative articles. Some may also offer additional benefits such as networking opportunities, discounts on goods and services, and even business and health insurance.

Find out if your industry has its own trade organization. In many cases, there may be several organizations to choose from. For example, I have the International Business Brokers Association at a national and international level but I also have a California Business Brokers Association.

If you aren't aware of associations in your field, start asking around. Make sure you evaluate the services provided by each organization and determine if the membership fee is worth the return on investment. Remember too that membership dues qualify as a business expense on your tax return.

If you've asked around and can't find an association, sit down with your computer and start doing a search. Just use key words as they relate to your industry followed by the word "association." You may be surprised at what you find. Once that is complete, do the same keyword search but replace the word association with conference. You may find some wonderful events to attend that can give you a huge and quick insight into your industry.

A couple of other reminders. Don't forget about your local Chamber of Commerce. This is an excellent place to receive support for your business and to network with business owners in your community.

There is also SCORE and Small Business Development Centers. Don't be afraid to give them a call or send them an email.

Evaluate Trade Associations

Use the template below to gather some information about associations or groups you think would be beneficial to you. There is a cost to join plus attending their events does require your time, so you need to be sure you are getting a good return on your investment.

List some associations for your industry and compare the benefits:

Association Name:	
Annual Fee:	
Number of Members:	
Regional Meetings?	
Annual Conference?	
Newsletter – Monthly or Quarterly?	
Benefits:	

Association Name:	
Annual Fee:	
Number of Members:	
Regional Meetings?	
Annual Conference?	
Newsletter – Monthly or Quarterly?	
Benefits:	

Association Name:	
Annual Fee:	
Number of Members:	
Regional Meetings?	
Annual Conference?	
Newsletter – Monthly or Quarterly?	
Benefits:	

Additional Sources Of Information

Attorney

American Bar Association   http://www.abanet.org/forums/franchising
Find a lawyer   http://www.lawyers.com
General Law questions   http://www.findlaw.com

Books

Small Business Books   http://www.smallbizbooks.com
Amazon   http://www.amazon.com
Borders   http://www.borders.com
Books Online   http://www.booksonline.com

Coaching/Knowledge

Business.com   http://www.business.com
Franklin Covey   https://www.franklincoveycoaching.com
The Alternative Board   http://www.tabboards.com
Society of Competitive Intelligence Professionals   http://www.scip.org

Franchise Association

International Franchise Association: http://www.franchise.org
Information on publicly traded franchises   http://www.edgar.gov

General Business Websites

Small Business Administration   http://sba.gov
IRS   http://www.irs.gov
Yahoo Finance   http://finance.yahoo.com
MSN Money   http://moneycentral.msn.com/home.asp
Stat-USA   http://www.stat-usa.gov
The Deal   http://www.thedeal.com
The Wall Street Journal   http://online.wsj.com/small-business
National Dialogue on Entrepreneurship   http://www.publicforuminstitute.org/nde

Leadership

Center for Entrepreneurial Leadership Clearinghouse on Entrepreneurial Education www.celcee.edu
CEO Express   http://www.ceoexpress.com/default.asp

Magazines

Inc. Magazine   http://www.inc.com
Success Magazine   http://www.success
Entrepreneur Magazine   http://www.entrepreneur.com
Forbes Magazine   http://www.forbes.com
Business Week   http://www.businessweek.com

Other Resources

Small Business Development Center (SBDC)

The Small Business Development Centers provide management assistance to small businesses. To find your local SBDC office, check here: http://sbdcnet.org/sbdc.php

SCORE - Service Corp Of Retired Executives (SCORE)

This national organization has local chapters full of experienced business professionals that have "been there, done that" and wish to give back to their local business community by providing a free consultation/mentoring service.

For more information about SCORE: http://www.score.org
To find a local chapter near you: http://www.score.org/explore_score.html

Chambers of Commerce

http://www.uschamber.com

The Learning Annex

http://www.learningannex.com

Business Publications

Business magazines provide interesting articles and resources for business owners. There is much you can learn from reading these inexpensive publications. Visit your local bookstore or library to see samples of the various magazines available and then subscribe to one or two of your favorites. Here are some publications to consider:

Entrepreneur Magazine: www.entrepreneur.som
Home Business Magazine: www.homebusinessmag.com
Small Business Opportunities: www.sbomag.com
Fortune Small Business (FSB):   www.fortune.com/fortune/smallbusiness
Inc. Magazine: www.inc.com

> *"Working hard overcomes a whole lot of other obstacles. You can have unbelievable intelligence, you can have connections, and you can have opportunities fall out of the sky. But in the end, hard work is the true, enduring characteristic of successful people."*
>
> *Rear Admiral Marsha Evans*

End Of Chapter Notes

Use this page to write down notes, ideas and other brainstorming for buying your business.

Glossary

The following glossary references some of the terms you may come across as you buy your franchise.

➢ **Account:** In the bookkeeping sense, account means a basic category of information in which the financial effects of transactions are recorded. For example, consider a checkbook. It provides an account or itemization of the cash inflows and outflows of the balance of your checking account such as health expense, rent expense, entertainment expense, cash, etc.

➢ **Accounting Method:** A process under which income and expenses are determined for tax purposes. This includes both the cash and accrual procedures.

➢ **Accounting Period:** The 12-month period that a taxpayer uses to determine federal income tax liability.

➢ **Accounts Payable (AP):** Amount of money owed to suppliers by the owner of the business that are not paid for by cash but on terms of credit agreed to by both parties.

➢ **Accounts Receivable (AR):** Amount of money owed by customers to the owner of the business that is not paid for by cash but on terms of credit agreed to by both parties.

➢ **Accrual Method of Accounting:** One of the two most common methods of accounting. Under this method, income is reported in the tax year earned, whether or not received, and deductions are claimed in the tax year incurred, whether or not paid.

➢ **Accrued Interest:** Interest that has been earned but not yet paid or credited.

➢ **Acknowledgement of Receipt definition:** The last page of an Offering Circular which indicates the receipt of the documents on a certain date. This, when signed and returned, acts as proof of the date one received the documents.

➢ **Advertising Fee:** Annual fee that is paid by the franchisee to the franchisor as his share of the corporate advertising expenditures. This advertising fee is charged by few franchisors only.

➢ **Agent:** Appointed individual who can act on behalf of the person or entity. The corporation is legally bound by the actions of the agent.

➢ **Amortization:** Similar to depreciation but applies to intangible assets such as leasehold improvements.

➢ **Approved Products:** Those products which a franchisee must buy from the franchisor. It also includes products which must be bought from approved suppliers. This is done by the franchisor in order to maintain quality across all franchisees.

➢ **Arbitration:** A way of resolving disputes by referring them to a third party which is selected by the parties.

➢ **Area Development Rights:** The rights allocated to a franchisee to operate a number of franchises within a specific geographic area.

➢ **Area Franchise:** A franchisee licensed to develop a particular area. This Area Franchisee sometimes includes performance targets and schedules. It can also include franchise sales rights.

➢ **Assignment Fees:** The monthly fees paid by the franchisee to the franchise company for expenses incurred by the company like corporate marketing and advertising.

➢ **Asset:** Anything owned that has economic value such as a truck, cash, inventory, etc.

- **Assumed Name:** *see DBA*

- **Balance Sheet (BS):** A statement of the financial status of the business on a certain date ("snapshot").

- **Basis:** The amount assigned to an asset from which gain or loss is determined for income tax purposes when the asset is sold. For assets acquired by purchase, this is the cost including other allowed adjustments such as depreciation.

- **Blue Sky:** That portion of a "claimed" value or requested price that cannot be supported or generally shown to exist through the application of established valuation methodology. Blue sky is different from Goodwill.

- **Book Value:** The depreciated value of an asset found on the balance sheet. This can be calculated by subtracting accumulated depreciation from the cost of the related asset.

- **Broker:** An intermediary between the buyer and the seller. He can represent either the buyer or the seller, and in some cases even both parties.

- **Business Format Franchise:** In Business Format Franchise the franchisor gives the permission to the franchisee for use of product, service and trademark. The entire business format is also taught to the franchisee including marketing, selling, inventory, accounting, and personnel procedures.

- **Capital Required:** The amount of cash one is required to have available.

- **Cash Basis Accounting:** A method of accounting wherein income and expenses are recognized, within the statements, when the business receives the income or pays the expense. *Also see Accrual Basis Accounting.*

- **Cash Flow:** Basically, the business' net income plus non-cash charges (depreciation, amortization, and depletion). It can be defined as before or after such items as taxes, debt service (interest only or principal and interest) or extraordinary items. (Should not be confused with Net Cash Flow, a.k.a. Free Cash Flow.)

- **Cash Method of Accounting:** One of the two most common methods of accounting with the other being Accrual. Under this method of accounting, income is reported in the tax year received and expenses are deducted in the tax year paid. *See Accrual Basis Accounting.*

- **Chart of Accounts:** The formal index of all the accounts used by the business to record its transactions.

- **Conversion Franchise:** A franchise system permitting existing businesses to join a national franchise system and be able to use its name, trademark and operating system.

- **Copyright:** Form of protection under the law for authors to protect "original works of authorship." This protection is available for both published and unpublished works.

- **Corporation:** A legal business entity owned by shareholders with the ability to own property, incur debts and sue or be sued. For income tax purposes, this term includes associations, trusts that have a majority of corporate characteristics, joint stock companies and insurance companies.

- **Cost of Goods Sold/Cost of Sales** (CGS, COGS, COS): A grouping of expenses applicable to the materials and labor incorporated directly in the goods or services delivered and sold.

- **DBA (Doing Business As):** An assumed name under which a business conducts business. For example, Billy Bob Enterprises, Inc. DBA Billy Bob's Hot Dog Grill and Bar.

- **Default:** The failure to perform as was agreed upon by the parties.

- **Depreciation:** The deduction of a reasonable allowance for the wear and tear of assets (excluding inventory) used in a trade or business or held for the production of income.

- **Disclosure:** Refers to revealing facts to others. In a franchise these facts may be complimentary to the franchisor, such as disclosing a prior bankruptcy or litigation.

- **Discretionary Earnings:** Adjusted earnings before taxes, interest income or expense, non-operating and non-recurring expenses, depreciation and other non-cash charges and prior to deducting an owners/officers compensation.

- **Distributorship:** The right granted by a manufacturer or a wholesaler for distribution or sale of products. Distributorship does not generally qualify as a franchisee. However, certain franchisees can qualify as a distributorship.

- **Domestic Corporation:** A corporation in the state where it has been incorporated.

- **Earnings Claims:** Assertions made by franchise companies of specific acquired sales levels or profitability levels.

- **EIN (Employer Identification Number):** *See Federal Tax Identification Number.*

- **Employee:** An individual that provides services to a business and is distinguished differently from an independent contractor. This is important because the withholding of incomes taxes on wage applies only to this individual.

- **Entrepreneur:** The Person who assumes the responsibility for organizing and operating the business. He also assumes the risk including the financial risk for a business venture.

- **Equity:** The recorded "value" of the ownership interest in a business entity. Also known as Owner's Equity.

- **Estimated (Useful) Life:** Period of time over which an asset will be used by a particular taxpayer.

- **Exclusive Territory:** Gives the right of the territory to the franchisee preventing the franchisor from appointing any other franchisee for the territory or carrying on business himself in the territory.

- **Expense:** An item charged against revenue in the income statement for something that is used up during the income statement period of time.

- **Fair Market Value (FMV):** The amount at which property would change hands between a willing buyer and a willing seller, neither being under compulsion to buy or sell and both having reasonable knowledge of the relevant facts.

- **Federal Tax Identification Number:** This is a number assigned to a corporation or other business entity by the federal government for tax purposes. This is also known as EIN (Employer Identification Number).

- **FICA (Federal Insurance Contributions Act):** The law that provides for Social Security and Medicare benefits. This program is financed by payroll taxes imposed equally on the employer and the employee. A person self-employed will pay both the employer and employee portion of this tax which is known as self-employment tax.

- **Fiscal Year:** Any period of exactly or approximately 12 months used by a business as its accounting period. Some retail businesses always close their year end on a Saturday and therefore will have either 52 or 53 weeks in a fiscal year.

- **Foreign Corporation:** A corporation not organized under the laws of one of the states or territories of the United States. This description relates to the federal level as this term is also used by each state to describe a corporation doing business in the state but organized under another states laws.

- **Franchise:** Permission given by a person or entity permitting the distribution of goods or services under his trademark, service mark or trade name by an agreement to another person or entity. During this period the grantor retains control over the franchisee.

- ➢ **Franchise Business Plan:** A strategic plan that lays down the company's objectives and the specific steps that need to be taken to achieve those objectives. The Business Plan is usually prepared by company management.

- ➢ **Franchise Fee:** Fee initially paid by the franchisee to the franchisor to acquire the franchise.

- ➢ **Goodwill:** The ability of a business to generate income in excess of a normal rate on assets due to superior managerial skills, market position, new product technology, etc.

- ➢ **Gross Profit:** That portion of Net Sales that remains after the subtraction of the Cost of Goods Sold. This is sometimes called Gross Margin.

- ➢ **Housemark:** A trademark which is used to identify the operations of an organization. This may in certain cases also be the company name. This trademark is used to identify one or more products and at times is used in combination with other trademarks.

- ➢ **Income:** All sources of business income; may be synonymous with Revenue or Sales.

- ➢ **Income Statement (IS):** A financial statement used to report the financial results of a business' operations during the period of time specified within the statement. Also known as the Profit and Loss or P&L.

- ➢ **Independent Contractor:** Taxpayer who contracts to do work according to his own methods and who is not subject to control except as to the results of such work. An employee, by contrast, is subject to the control of the employer as to the methods to be used to obtain the desired results.

- ➢ **Industry:** The category of business to which a franchise belongs. It is an all-encompassing area of business that can incorporate several different sectors.

- ➢ **Intangible Personal Property:** Assets, other than real property, with no intrinsic value; their value lies in the rights conveyed. Examples include cash, insurance, stock, goodwill, and patents.

- ➢ **International Franchise Association (IFA):** Based in Washington, D.C., a trade association for franchisors.

- ➢ **Inventory:** List of articles of property. For income tax purposes, this refers only to a list of articles comprising stock in trade–articles held for sale to customers in the regular course of a trade or business.

- ➢ **Lessee:** One who rents property from another. In the case of real estate, the lessee is also known as the tenant.

- ➢ **Lessor:** One who rents property to another. In the case of real estate, the lessor is also known as the landlord.

- ➢ **Limited Liability Company (LLC):** Operating structure contains the liability protection of a corporation and the flexibility of a partnership.

- ➢ **Liquidation:** The process of converting securities or other property into cash.

- ➢ **Marketing Plan:** Detailed plan setting the marketing activities of the organization.

- ➢ **Master Franchise:** Individual or a company which owns the exclusive rights to develop a particular geographic area.

- ➢ **NAICS (North American Industry Classification System) Code:** A system of numbering that assigns a unique number to each business industry and thereby allows for collection and comparison of statistical information within an industry. *Also see SIC code.*

- ➢ **Operations Manual:** Covers all the aspects of the business and consists of guidelines for the franchisee on how to operate the franchised business.

- **Ownership:** A generic term meaning 100% controlling ownership.

- **Partnership:** Form of business in which two or more persons join their money and skills in conducting the business. This form is treated as a conduit and is not subject to taxation.

- **Patent:** Legal protection for an inventor. If issued, a patent grants "the right to exclude others from making, using, offering for sale, or selling" the invention. There are three types of patents: design, utility and plant.

- **Perquisites (Perks):** Special additional benefits received as compensation because of position. In privately held businesses these are often a result of the ability of the business to pay for them, more than a result of market rate compensation for the services provided to the business. For example, company-paid vehicles, insurance, travel, memberships, etc.

- **Prepaid Expense:** The capitalized payment for items such as rent, insurance, etc. that cover more than one year. Cash-basis as well as accrual-basis taxpayers usually are required to capitalize these types of costs.

- **Product Format Franchise:** Where the franchised product or service does not constitute the majority of the products or services on offer by the franchisee.

- **Pro forma statements:** Statements issued by the franchisor to the franchisee based on actual operating results of the franchisor's units or franchise establishments. It can be in the form of any statement which measures profits and expenses.

- **Protected Territory:** Territory allotted to a franchisee where the franchisor has promised not to franchise to another franchisee or open a company owned business.

- **Public Figure Involvement:** When a public figure is endorsing a franchised product then the nature of the agreement between the public figure and the franchisor must be disclosed.

- **Qualification Questionnaire:** Document prepared by the franchisor to seek information from a prospective franchise.

- **Quality Control:** The method used by the franchisor to enforce the rules set in the operating manuals. Quality control involves regional coordinators visiting each franchisee.

- **Royalty:** The franchisee is required to pay to the franchisor a percentage of the gross sales on a monthly basis.

- **S Corporation:** An elective provision permitting certain small business corporations and their shareholders to elect special income tax treatment. Of major significance is the fact that this election usually avoids the corporate income tax and corporate losses can be claimed by the shareholders.

- **Section 179 Expense Deduction:** An election to treat the cost of certain qualified property as a currently deductible expense rather than as a capital expenditure. This treatment is also referred to as expensing. A maximum deduction, adjusted annually, may be claimed for qualified assets placed in service during the year. This deduction may be further limited based on the total cost of depreciable assets placed in service during the year.

- **Sector:** The categories included within a broader scope of franchise opportunities. It is also known as the Industry.

- **SIC (Standard Industrial Classification) Code or NAICS (North American Industry Classification System) Code:** System of numbering that assigns a unique number to each business industry. This allows for collection and comparison of statistical information within an industry.

- **Slick:** Pre-paid piece of advertising material which the franchisor gives to the franchisee for use in local print media.

> **Source Documents:** Virtually every business transaction needs documentation which is known as a source document or supporting documentation (back-up). Examples include check register, invoice, receipt, purchase order, etc.

> **Start-up Costs:** The investment required to be made by the franchisee at the start of the franchise.

> **Total Investment:** Initial investment, the working capital, and subsequent additions to inventory and equipment which will be necessary for the fully operational and profitable enterprise.

> **Trade Secret:** Are revealed to the franchisee by the franchise transaction.

> **Trademark:** Word, name, symbol, or device that is used in trade with goods to indicate the source of the goods and to distinguish them from the goods of others.

> **Turnkey:** The franchisor is expected to provide the platform to run the business to the franchisee, even without any input from the franchisee.

> **Working Capital:** Excess of the value of the current assets over the value of the current liabilities.

Other Books In This Series

If you are considering business ownership there are three options available to you. Start your own business from scratch, buy an existing business or buy the rights to a franchise in your local market. This 144 page guide is for those who are considering buying a franchise. The processes can be very confusing and demanding trying to work out the many variables such as which franchise to buy, what franchises are available, what is the initial cost, how much are the royalties and any other ongoing costs and which legal entity to use. It also looks at getting a loan, what the franchisor provides, your role, how much and what sort of support you get. This guide covers all these questions and many more. If you are serious about buying a franchise this guide will walk you through the steps and provide the answers for you from the initial steps to opening the doors of your business while answering all your questions so you do things from a position of strength.

Are you considering business ownership and not sure where to start? If so, you have three options. Buy an existing business, buy the rights to a franchise or start your own business from scratch. This 182 page workbook includes how to decide which industry is right for you, how to create your legal entity, obtain business permits and licenses and business insurance. It also explains how to build your dream business using the solid foundations of a business plan, sales and marketing plan and productivity plan, all dovetailed with financial planning tools such as start up costs planners, profit and loss projectors, sales forecasts, break even analysis and more. It also includes finance options, checklists, resources, other planning sheets and tools to start your business as quickly as possible. Finally, this workbook shows how to do all this and more with the focus that a buyer may wish to buy your business and if so, what processes you would follow to sell for the highest price.

Thinking about selling your business? This 150 page comprehensive workbook helps you understand the many complexities and decisions you have to make. Written by a professional business broker with many years of real world business experience, this guide shows you how to sell your business in the shortest possible time for the best possible price. It includes reasons why you need to plan ahead for taxes, how to avoid potential legal, accounting, and other roadblocks, how to value your business and other assets, the different types of professionals available and how to research and properly prepare for selling. Also includes how to search for and qualify potential buyers, address finance concerns, protect you and your business with confidentiality agreements, prepare an executive summary, confidential business review and conduct effective negotiations. Also includes dozens of worksheets, checklists, and charts for you to track during the steps to sell.

About The Author

Andrew Rogerson currently holds the Certified Business Intermediary (CBI) designation from the International Business Brokers Association (IBBA), the highest designation awarded by the IBBA. Andrew has also earned the Certified Business Broker (CBB) designation from the California Association of Business Brokers. He holds a Certified Machinery and Equipment designation (CMEA) from the National Business and Builders Institute and is a Certified Senior Business Analyst (CSBA) with the Society of Business Analysts. He also holds a Broker's License with the California Department of Real Estate.

As the owner and managing director of Rogerson Business Services in Sacramento, CA, Andrew assists his clients with both selling and buying businesses.

Since 1983, Andrew has owned and operated five businesses. At just 27 years old, he bought his first business, an international travel agency. With hard work resulting in increased sales, Andrew sold the travel agency just two years later for 2 1/2 times his original purchase price.

Andrew's next venture involved owning and managing two retail office equipment/furniture stores, followed by a wholesale travel and tourism company based in Los Angeles that had an annual turnover of $10,000,000. More recently, Andrew and his wife Anne owned an executive suites business in Fair Oaks, CA. Anne operated this business while Andrew worked as an outsourced program manager at the Roseville campus of Hewlett Packard. At HP, Andrew managed a team of 42 employees, deploying a new global call center and support team that included Web developers, technical writers and trainers.

Andrew was educated at La Trobe University in Melbourne, Australia, his native country, and recently completed studies in Business Valuation and Appraisals and Business Brokerage. Andrew and Anne have two daughters, Belinda and Catherine and reside in Sacramento, California. Andrew enjoys flying (he is pursuing his pilot's license) and SCUBA diving as well as sports and politics.

Contact Andrew for Assistance with Buying or Selling a Business

Andrew offers a broad range of services including business valuations, transaction analysis, consulting for business sellers and buyers, consulting for buyers considering franchise ownership and appraisals for machinery and equipment.

The combination of Andrew's hands-on experience in the business buying and selling process, his diverse background in a variety of industries and his international business experience makes him an ideal choice for a business intermediary.

Call Andrew Rogerson at (916) 570-2674 or send him an e-mail at info@Andrew-Rogerson.com to discuss how you can put his knowledge and experience to work for you.

Visit Andrew's website: www.Andrew-Rogerson.com